Hawks on Hawks

Hawks on Hawks

Joseph McBride

foreword by Quentin Tarantino

faber and faber
LONDON · BOSTON

First published in Great Britain in 1996
by Faber and Faber Limited
3 Queen Square London WC1N 3AU

Photoset by Parker Typesetting Service, Leicester
Printed in England by Clays Ltd, St Ives plc

Originally published in the USA in 1982 by The University of California Press

A CIP record for this book is available from the British Library

ISBN 0–571–17700–X

2 4 6 8 10 9 7 5 3 2

To Jessica

Howard Winchester Hawks (1896–1977)

Contents

Introduction

The distinctive signature of Howard Hawks appeared on several dozen of the most popular movies ever made in Hollywood. The most versatile of all great American directors, he worked with equal ease in screwball comedies, westerns, gangster movies, musicals, private-eye melodramas, and adventure films. He made some of the best movies of such male stars as John Wayne, Humphrey Bogart, Cary Grant, and Gary Cooper, and his portrayals of tough, sexy, sophisticated women such as Lauren Bacall, Carole Lombard, Rosalind Russell, and Angie Dickinson were far ahead of their time. He collaborated with a remarkable array of first-rate writers, including Ernest Hemingway and William Faulkner. As a flyer, hunter, fisherman, automobile racer, horseman, and all-around *bon vivant*, he lived a colourful life that could have been taken straight from one of his own movies. Hawks's work has grown in stature with the years, and his movies seem as fresh and lively today as when they were made. Contemporary audiences delight in revivals of such Hawks classics as *Scarface*, *Twentieth Century*, *Bringing Up Baby*, *Only Angels Have Wings*, *His Girl Friday*, *To Have and Have Not*, *The Big Sleep*, *Red River*, *Gentlemen Prefer Blondes*, and *Rio Bravo*. When he was honoured in 1975 with an Oscar for his six decades in films, the Academy of Motion Picture Arts and Sciences cited him as 'a giant of the American cinema whose pictures, taken as a whole, represent one of the most consistent, vivid, and varied bodies of work in world cinema'.

Until his late years, however, Hawks was never given much serious attention. He was always known in Hollywood as a reliable director-producer with deft technical skills, a keen storytelling sense, an eye for new talent, and an unerring instinct for the box office. But he never courted prestige by making self-consciously 'important'

1 Hawks and McBride at the Laguna Beach seminar 22 October 1977.

pictures. He contented himself with making the kind of straightfor-
ward, enjoyable, unpretentious stories that he liked and that the
audience liked. Hawks was both bemused and gratified at the surge
of attention paid him in the 1960s and 1970s, when the new
generation of young film buffs and film-makers, led by the
influential figures of the French New Wave, discovered him and
championed his ability to bring personal expression to commercial
film-making. Looking back over his long career, which began in the
silent era and continued through 1970, they found a remarkable
consistency of theme and personality in what had appeared to
casual moviegoers as a random assortment of genre pieces.

Hawks's films almost always deal with a tightly knit group of
professionals trying to perform a difficult task together while
upholding their own rigorously defined code of conduct. Whether
they are gunfighters, aviators, hunters, detectives, newspapermen,
or scientists, Hawks's people function in a self-enclosed society in
which the standards of personal conduct are professional skill,

group loyalty, and self-respect. The highest accolade one Hawks character can pay another is 'You did a good job,' and the worst thing one can say of another is 'He just wasn't good enough.'

If Hawks is, as Jacques Rivette wrote in the first major essay on Hawks's work, 'the only American director who knows how to draw a moral' ('The Genius of Howard Hawks', *Focus on Howard Hawks*, p. 73), the morality of his characters is not a matter of their adherence to abstract social or ethical precepts but an existential morality, a function of their behaviour towards each other. A typical plot mechanism in a Hawks film is the struggle of a flawed character (e.g., Richard Barthelmess in *Only Angels Have Wings*, Walter Brennan in *To Have and Have Not*, Dean Martin in *Rio Bravo*) to prove himself worthy of respect by the rest of the group, by overcoming tendencies to disloyalty, cowardice, physical disability, or immaturity. Not even the strongest characters in Hawks's films can function effectively outside the group: though John Wayne's Sheriff John T. Chance stoically tries to reject the help of friends all the way through *Rio Bravo*, his ultimate survival depends on their intercession in his behalf. Though Hawks's characters often act in positions of social responsibility, they typically maintain an aloof, isolated group identity within the general society, which enters into the stories only tangentially, as a hostile force challenging the unity of the group and its self-sustaining value system.

Despite the underlying seriousness of Hawks's concerns, his films rarely express their themes in a solemn or heavy-handed manner. Indeed, it is a much remarked-upon paradox of his work that his dramatic films are often even funnier than his actual comedies. All his films have a large component of playful humour, reflecting Hawks's enjoyment of good fellowship, the pleasure he takes in seeing a job well done, and the importance he places on balancing professional danger with recuperative relaxation. His sense of humour is more than just a function of his desire to be entertaining: it is an essential part of his view of human existence. Comedy and tragedy are interrelated in his work, the drama often coming from a character overcoming tendencies to ridiculousness, and the comedy typically arising from the descent of a dignified person into absurdity. Hawks expresses his morality through his comic perspective: when a Hawks character behaves either with undue self-importance or with a lack of self-respect, he exposes himself to mockery. Hawks's guiding principle, as Molly Haskell defined it in her excellent essay on the director in *Cinema: A Critical Dictionary*, is 'the picture of man poised, comically or heroically, against an antagonistic nature, a nothingness as devoid of meaning as Samuel Beckett's, but determined not the less to act out his destiny, to assert mind against mindlessness' (p. 474).

Hawks's work can be faulted for its narrowness of thematic range, in contrast to the breadth of vision one finds in the work of Renoir or Ford or Rossellini, and the lack of thematic development in his work over such a long career is evidence of a self-centred, relatively unquestioning personality. But if these limitations prevent Hawks from reaching the highest level of cinematic greatness, they must also be recognized as essential elements in his artistic strength. Like his utilitarian visual style, which avoids superfluous flourishes to concentrate on presenting a scene in the clearest and most economical way, Hawks's thematic simplicity enabled him to concentrate on nuances of human behaviour with a rare degree of richness and complexity.

John Belton's essay, 'Hawks and Co.', in *Focus on Howard Hawks*, describes Hawks's use of gestures to create characterization and rightly places primary importance on the physical immediacy, rather than the abstract thematic values, of his work. Verbalizing Hawks's themes has a tendency to make them sound puerile, but a close viewing of his work makes it clear that his greatness was in his ability to make people come alive on screen. We understand his themes through the complexity of his people, rather than seeing his people as reductive illustrations of his themes. And though he is often misleadingly categorized as an 'action' director, probably because of the genres in which he chose to work, Hawks showed remarkably little interest in action for its own sake; he should more accurately be placed alongside behaviouristic directors such as Ozu, McCarey, and Rohmer in his intimate concentration on the subtleties of character as revealed through the texture of dialogue and physical expressiveness.

Manny Farber, the first American critic to write perceptively on

Hawks, wrote in 'Howard Hawks', his 1969 overview of Hawks's career:

No artist is less suited to a discussion of profound themes than Hawks, whose attraction to strutting braggarts, boyishly cynical dialogue, and melodramatic fiction always rests on his poetic sense of action. It would be impossible to find anything profound in Rosalind Russell's Hildy (in His Girl Friday), *but there is a magic in the mobile unity of the woman: her very mannish pinstripe suits, the highly stylized way she plants a hand on her hip, and her projecting of the ultimate in sophisticated swagger, taking off her hat and coat and showing how a real reporter sets up shop. The genius of such action engineering is that Hawks is able to poeticize dialogue as well as faces and costume, making a 100 per cent ordinary line – Hildy's parting shot to Earl Williams in his death cell: 'Goodbye, Earl, and good luck' – seem to float in an air of poignant, voluptuous cynicism* (Focus on Howard Hawks, *pp. 33–34*).

When Hawks was confronted with questions about his intentions in creating such-and-such a scene, he would almost invariably reply with an anecdote illuminating *how* he created the scene rather than what it was supposed to mean. He often expressed surprise and amusement at the things people were finding in his work, at the deep levels of meaning and symbolism critics were unearthing in what seemed to him to be 'just good stories'. But while he was inclined to be sarcastic about the more arcane critical pieces written about him, he was obviously pleased to find that the care and energy he had devoted to his work were finally being appreciated. He often told his young questioners, 'You fellows know more about my work than I do.'

When I served as moderator of an audience discussion with Hawks during a retrospective of his work in 1974 at the Los Angeles County Museum of Art, he chose to start off the evening by recalling the title of one article about him in an American film magazine of the mid-1960s: 'Who The Hell is Howard Hawks?' After calling me up to join him at the microphone, Hawks wondered if I had written the article (I hadn't), and then he jokingly demanded, 'Now maybe you could tell *me*.'

Hawks's attitude was partly a pose. Like many directors of his generation, he preferred to present himself as a craftsman rather than as an artist. But his disinclination to expound on the thematic intentions of his work should not be taken as a true measure of his self-awareness as a film-maker.

François Truffaut, the French director and critic who conducted a landmark book-length interview with Alfred Hitchcock in the mid-1960s, told me in 1974 that he wished a similar book could be done with Hawks. 'Something I feel that's very interesting with Hawks,' Truffaut said on another occasion,

> is that in all those interviews, he always criticizes, he raps the intellectuals, and in my opinion he is one of the most intellectual film-makers in America. He often speaks in terms of film concepts. He has many general theories. He doesn't belong to the school of instinctive film-makers. He thinks of everything he does, everything is thought out. So somebody ought to tell him one day that despite himself he is an intellectual and that he has to accept that. (Grand Illusions, Winter 1977, pp. 31–32)

As I hope this book will show, Hawks's anecdotes often illustrated complex points more succinctly than critics are able to do with reams of windy analysis. He was endlessly tractable and informative on questions of technique and story construction, and his analyses of actors' personalities were brilliantly insightful, as one might expect from the superb performances he evoked. When goaded into more theoretical discussion, he replied with clear and direct statements which, while not as expansive and analytical as one might wish, were forceful elucidations of the moral and aesthetic principles by which he worked. Listening to Hawks discuss his working methods was the equivalent of attending a master class in the *practical* art of film direction.

Oddly enough, when Truffaut suggested to me that somebody should do a book on Hawks comparable to his book on Hitchcock, I was then in the process of doing just such a book without realizing it. I first met Hawks in November 1970, at the Chicago Film Festival, a month before the première of what would turn out to be his last film, *Rio Lobo*. After transcribing and publishing his discussion with the audience at the festival, I edited a book of articles on him as *Focus on Howard Hawks* in 1972. Then I moved from the Midwest to California, and over the next few years I visited Hawks frequently at his home in Palm Springs, spending long afternoons taping discussions with him about his films. I was doing it purely for my own enjoyment and instruction – or so I thought.

Having a book on his movies published led to the opportunity of moderating several panel discussions with Hawks in Southern California. His daughter Barbara, who attended some of those sessions, quipped that Hawks and I were beginning to resemble a vaudeville team, with me feeding him straight lines and him responding on cue as if he'd never heard the questions before. And as luck would have it, I had the chance for one last, exhaustive interview session with Hawks over a three-day period in the fall of 1977, just two months before his death, when the Directors Guild of America and the Los Angeles Cinematheque asked me to moderate a 'Weekend with Howard Hawks and His Films' in Laguna Beach. By that time it had dawned on me that all the talking I'd been doing with Hawks over the last seven years was adding up to a thorough reminiscence and analysis of his career. I deliberately used the Laguna Beach weekend to explore areas that remained to be covered in his work, and when it was all over I had the interview book that Truffaut had suggested needed to be done.

No one could have guessed that Hawks's career was ending when we first met in Chicago. He was then almost seventy-four years of age, but he looked about fifty. John Ford, clearly envious of Hawks's ease with the ladies, used to call him 'the goddam grey fox of Brentwood', and Ben Hecht described him in his autobiography, *A Child of the Century*, as 'the drawling fashion plate Howard Hawks, a-purr with melodrama'. He still fit those descriptions. Everyone agreed that Hawks was a supremely stylish man: tall, lean, dapper, dressed with conservative elegance, eyes veiled behind dark aviator glasses, cordial but reserved, in total appearance a man who commanded instant respect. As the director Don Siegel once observed of Hawks, 'He looks like a director, he acts like a director, he talks like a director, and he's a damn good director.'

Into his eighties, Hawks continued to give the impression that a life of disciplined work and vigorous play was going to keep him strong and dignified and alert while other men of his generation were declining into decrepitude. His daughter told me shortly after his death, 'We thought he would live forever – it was as if he had beaten the system.' When I left Hawks's home after one of our visits, which seldom lasted less than five hours, *I* always felt exhausted, and *he* always looked great. It never occurred to me that one day it would no longer be possible to pick up the phone, call Hawks in Palm Springs (always at the last minute, because he didn't like to make plans in advance), and drive down to spend an afternoon chatting with him. It still seems hard to realize I can't do that.

Hawks seemed to be in an especially kindly, good-humoured, mellow mood that last time I saw him, and the intimacy of the experience we all shared at the resort hotel made us feel the same kind of relaxed camaraderie Hawks created in his films. The occasional bitterness I had detected in him during his last years of not-quite-voluntary retirement seemed to have given way to a final serenity. 'I've had a hell of a good life,' he said shortly before his death. Hearing him tell his favourite stories one last time, and seeing the affectionate and enthusiastic response of the youthful audience to him and his films, brought alive to me a full awareness of Hawks's stature in the history of the American cinema.

This book is drawn from nine separate discussions with Hawks from 1970 through 1977. They took place at the Chicago Film Festival in November 1970; at the Los Angeles County Museum of Art in February 1974; at Sherwood Oaks Experimental College in Hollywood in May 1974; at Hawks's home in Palm Springs in February and August 1974, and in April 1975; and at the Surf and Sand Hotel in Laguna Beach on October 21–23, 1977. I have edited the transcripts freely, rearranging questions and answers into a continuous narrative of Hawks's career. The order is largely chron-ological, although general remarks on some major collaborators and on topics such as writing and acting and camerawork have been grouped together in separate chapters. Hawks was fond of repeating and refining stories in his interviews (as, indeed, he was in his film work), so I had the opportunity of hearing him tell several of his favourite stories on numerous occasions. I have edited each of these together to make up the most complete and entertaining versions.

2 Hawks and his daughter Barbara on location for *The Big Sky*.

Like a Hawks film, this book was a group effort. I would like to thank the people who joined me in some of these discussions, including Gerald Peary, Patrick McGilligan, Peter Bogdanovich, Alex Ameripoor, and the audiences who asked questions at the events I moderated. Though this book contains much material never before published, portions of some interviews have appeared in *Sight and Sound*, *Film Comment*, *Focus on Howard Hawks*, and the DGA pamphlet *Howard Hawks: A Weekend with the Director and His Films*, and the editors' permission to reprint is gratefully acknowledged. Thanks also for permission to make use of unedited transcripts made by institutions mentioned above, and to David Shepard, Tee Bosustow, Lee Atwell, Gary Shusett, Ronald Haver, Joan Cohen, Elizabeth Dalton, James D'Arc, Rafe Blasi, Ed and Sherall Scharlach, François Truffaut, Robin Wood, and Barbara Hawks McCampbell, for their assistance in preparing this book. I would also like to acknowledge the cooperation of Todd McCarthy, who participated in the Laguna Beach discussions and later exchanged information with me from his research on Hawks.

xvii

1

Storytelling

All I'm doing is telling a story. I don't analyse or do a lot of thinking about it. I work on the fact that if I like somebody and think they're attractive, I can make them attractive. If I think a thing's funny, then people laugh at it. If I think a thing's dramatic, the audience does. I'm very lucky that way. I don't stop to analyse it. We just made scenes that were fun to do. I think our job is to make entertainment.

You say that you are an entertainer, but critics in the last few years have been treating you as something more than that. Do you think they're right?
Oh, I listen to them, and I get open-mouthed and wonder where they find some of the stuff that they say about me. I'm very glad that they like it, and I'm very glad that a lot of them are copying what I do, but they find things. They give me credit for an awful lot of things that I don't pay any attention to.

Do all good directors have a personal style?
The men that I think are good directors certainly have a style. I can go and tell who directed it. If you were listening to a comedian tell a joke, you'd certainly know the way Bob Hope tells it, and you can just go right down the line – everybody has his own particular way of telling his story, and I think if a director's any good he's got his own way of telling it.

Your films always have a very solid structure. But in today's films it almost seems unfashionable to have one.
Well, if they let those fellows that are making them today go on with no structure, when they make the second or third picture I think they'll begin to learn that they better have a little structure. We made

3 Bogart (as detective Philip Marlowe) in *The Big Sleep*.

a picture that worked pretty well called *The Big Sleep*, and I never figured out what was going on, but I thought that the basic thing had great scenes in it, and it was good entertainment. After that got by, I said, 'I'm never going to worry about being logical again.' But in some of today's pictures, you don't know where you are, who's talking, or anything, and that's why they've got motion pictures lying around in Hollywood that they can't make head or tail out of. A director's a storyteller, and if he tells a story that people can't understand, then he shouldn't be a director. I don't care what they do as long as they can tell it well. We haven't run out of stories.

2

Beginnings

Could you tell me about your family and your early years?
We moved from Indiana to Neenah, Wisconsin, when I was about
two years old. My father, my grandfather, and my uncle all had
paper mills. Then due to my mother's health we came to California
when I was ten years old. We lived in Pasadena. My father was vice-
president of a hotel company that owned a bunch of the big hotels
up in San Francisco. And then we had an orange grove in Glendora.
I went to some high school in Glendora and to a fine school in
Pasadena called Throop that taught woodworking and metalwork-
ing; it was where anybody went who was going to study
engineering. [Hawks attended Throop Polytechnic Institute for a
year of elementary school and a year of high school.] I went to
Exeter to prep school and then to Cornell University.

Is it true that the story of your film Come and Get It *was based on
your grandfather?*
Yes, well, it was based on about four men. She [Edna Ferber, who
wrote the novel] took parts from each man. They were all big
lumber men. She was a clerk in a five-and-ten-cent store or
something like that in Appleton, Wisconsin. I started talking with
Edna Ferber, and she said, 'How come you know so much about it?'
And I said, 'Well, my grandfather's the one you're writing about.'
'Oh, my God!' she said. I said, 'I want to change some of your stuff,'
and she said, 'Change it. I won't worry a bit.'

Was your grandfather in the mould of the John Wayne tough guy?
He had a great deal more sense of humour than John.

3

Really bold people predominate in your films. I get the feeling that you have a fascination with the pioneer spirit and with the people who had the boldness to go out there and carve the wilderness. Is that part of your family heritage, perhaps?
I don't think it's family heritage. It's just that I like those people and they're easy for me to make scenes about. It's easy for me to make stuff about flyers because I've done so much flying.

Have you ever put other members of your family into a movie besides your grandfather?
I put my grandmother in. Whenever she was happy, she started to cry. She'd say, 'I'm so happy!' and start to cry. She was a marvellous character. And I've used things about everybody. There are a lot of incidents that have happened or that I've seen happen that I've used in pictures. That's where you get them.

I've seen people die, you know. I've been mixed up in a lot of things, flying, racing, stuff like that. A director can tell the stories best that he knows. Well. I saw a fellow die once. He was in a plane wreck with his best friend. He said, 'I feel kinda funny.' The guy said, 'Your neck's broken.' He was very quiet and he said, 'I've thought for a long time just how I'd act when it was all over. I don't know how good I'm going to be.' And the friend said, 'Do you mean you want to see it out?' And he said, 'Yeah.' So we all left and he died. I used that in *Only Angels Have Wings*. I used it again in *Rio Lobo*. That's a good dying.

Could you tell me about your brother Kenneth?
For brothers we get along very well. I was national junior champion in tennis, and he was intercollegiate champion. Ken was awful good; he beat [Bill] Tilden four weeks before Tilden won at Forest Hills. We used to play every day with two world's champions, Maurie McLoughlin and Tom Bundy. We were the only competition they could get in Santa Monica. I helped my brother get started as a director. He did a pretty good job with his first picture [*Big Time*, 1929], and then when he was doing his second picture he was killed [in the aerial collision of two camera planes on 2 January 1930, during the filming of *Such Men Are Dangerous*].

4

What kind of director do you think he would have developed into?
Well, he seemed to be developing into a fellow who was much warmer than I was – a little bit more like Frank Borzage was, that kind of picture.

How old were you when you were a race-car driver?
Oh, seventeen or eighteen, somewhere around there. I raced cars for about three years, did my own work on them, and built a car that won Indianapolis. I won quite a few races because I had a better car than the other fellow had. This was a Mercedes that my grandfather gave me. I had a sort of partner, and he had a great big chain-driven Fiat. It had a great deal more power, but it didn't handle as well. We raced on dirt tracks. It wasn't very polite racing. If you could shove somebody through a fence you did it. I met Victor Fleming [director of *Gone With the Wind* and *The Wizard of Oz*] driving in a race. I put him through a fence and wrecked his car. I won the race and saw him coming; I thought I was gonna have a fight with him. Instead of that, he came up with a grin and he said, 'That was pretty good, but don't ever try it again, because I'll just run into you.' We became very good friends. He came up to my house for a while when he was looking for a place, and he stayed five years.

Did you share the same girlfriends, like the characters in your movies?
Not for long.

Did you have any bad accidents while racing?
Oh, no, just a broken leg.

Did your family ever try to steer you toward any kind of profession?
No, I wanted to be an engineer. I went to school where I wanted to; my whole family seems to do that. I went to Cornell, my brothers went to Yale, my son went to Princeton. In the summer, to make some money, I worked at Famous Players-Lasky Studio [then the production arm of Paramount]. I was sort of an assistant property man. Douglas Fairbanks was making a picture, and he wanted a modern set, a modern apartment. Nobody knew what the hell a

5

modern thing was, but I had studied about five or six years of architecture, and I knew, so I said, 'Oh, I can do that.' Doug said he liked it, and he and I became friends. He was courting Mary [Pickford] at the time, and so Mary made me her property man. I think principally because I could get them both to go to work when they were in their bungalow. Then she moved me up to assistant director. And one day [on *The Little Princess*, 1917, directed by Marshall Neilan] the director got drunk, and Mary said, 'I guess we can't work.' I said, 'Why don't we make some scenes?' She said, 'Can you do it?' and I said, 'Yeah.' I made some, and she liked it very much.

Do you remember what your first moment as a director was like?
She played a dual role, and she said, 'I wish I could follow myself into the room.' We drew a blank after she entered the room, crossed the film behind her, then rewound it and let her come in. And it happened that they matched. The cameraman was just sweating because he said it's only one chance in ten that it'll match. But it worked beautifully, and she was so pleased. And I remember another scene where she wished that a doll could come into the room; it was a fantasy, you know, one would talk to her. 'Well,' I said, 'we can do that.' We put soft solder in the arms and legs of the doll, and we made it so we could move it by stop-motion a little ways at a time. You didn't really direct Mary. She was a very sure person in her own category. But I made the scenes. Then the war came along, and I got quite a little bit of notoriety because she came up on a bond drive and said she would come out to where our squadron was training and I could take her around. So, holy smoke, officers and colonels, everybody like that was wondering what the devil the private was doing with Mary.

What kind of experiences did you have during the war?
There wasn't very much. We went through what they called ground school. I was commander of a squadron. While I was waiting to be called I went out and got about an hour's experience flying. And then when we got down to flying school I think I got about an hour and three-quarters flying, and they made me an instructor. Nobody

flew in those days; nobody knew how to. And it was awfully slow because there were two thousand cadets down there [in Texas] and only seven airplanes. I remember one time the colonel came out, we were all digging post holes, and he said, 'What are you doing, young men?' And one guy said, 'Learning to fly, sir.' They threw him in the brig for doing it. The chance of getting into combat was very futile, and I went into a course in big gun spotting, flying and spotting artillery shelters. I had a hell of a time getting sent to the spotting place because they wanted me as an instructor. Then the war was over.

Silent Films

I started as property man about the same time Jimmy Wong Howe started as an assistant cameraman. And the first thing he did – we all made our dissolves in the camera, you know, you started to dissolve at footage number 275, and you were out at 285 – well, he erased all those numbers on a DeMille picture. I was property man for Cecil DeMille, and I was supposed to jump on top of a conference table when a bomb in the war hit the chateau, and I was supposed to drop plaster on everything. They set off the bomb, and it was about six buckets of flash powder – I was under a canvas and I couldn't breathe, so I fell under the conference table, and Jimmy and I got together and decided that we'd picked a pretty hard business.

You directed a couple of short comedies before you became a feature director. Do those still exist?
Christ, I don't know.

How did you get to make them?
I knew Jack Warner – he was just beginning, didn't have too much money in those days. And I think that I loaned Warner some money. So he said, 'Would you like to make some comedies?' And I said sure. I made three or four of them, I don't remember how many, and then I got bored with doing them.

Who was in them?
The star was Monty Banks. I named him – his name was Mario Bianchi – and Monty Banks married Gracie Fields and became a multi-millionaire. He got fifty dollars a week. One time he got fresh, so I put a ladder up to the house and had him climb into the chimney. He got all covered with black soot, and he got down on his

knees and begged me to let him back. So we let him back, but I always kept the ladder around. The girl was Alice Terry, who married Rex Ingram and became quite a big star.

Do you remember the titles of those pictures?
God, no.

Do you remember anything else about the shooting?
Oh, I remember that I used to drive automobiles in stunts. Tipped over on the wheels, skidded, drove into poles. I did everything in the pictures. The budget was only three thousand dollars.

Were they successful?
Yeah, very successful. I got my training making those one-reelers. A lot of people – Frank Capra, George Stevens, even Cary Grant – we all trained making one-reel pictures. We had thorough comedy training.

Were you doing them in the hope of becoming a feature director?
I don't remember that. I didn't feel I knew enough about directing pictures. I finally got tired of other people directing and me writing, so I went to see a movie every night for six months. And if I thought the movie was worth studying, I saw it twice that same night until I felt that I knew enough to direct. I learned right in the beginning from Jack Ford, and I learned what not to do by watching Cecil DeMille.

You produced features independently before you went back to Famous Players-Lasky.
Yeah, I got Mickey Neilan, Allan Dwan, Allen Holubar, they were the best directors in the picture business. We made a lot of money the first year, then all of them got a girl. That was the downfall. We lost all the money the next year. Dwan got a redhead who couldn't act. Marvellous gal, good-looking, lots of fun and everything, she couldn't act at all.

One of those movies you produced was Quicksands [*1923; the story, written by Hawks, dealt with the US Army chasing dope smugglers along the Mexican border*].

We made that for $18,000 down in Mexico. Jack Conway was the director. Richard Dix and Helene Chadwick were in the picture. I had two stuntmen who got five dollars a day, Richard Arlen and Eddie Sutherland. When we were down there making the picture, the Tenth Cavalry fed us and housed us and gave us two thousand men. The Tenth Cavalry was a Negro cavalry that chased Pancho Villa. I made a one-day history of the regiment for them. We used all of our cameras, and three of us – the assistant director and production manager, and an actor – we all made different scenes. I think I made the ones where they were chasing Villa. In *Quicksands*, we had all of the heavies in a room with the girl and the Tenth Cavalry coming to the rescue. And the prop man was using wax bullets, but the wax was so old it was really doing damage. One fellow got shot and spit out the bullet, and one other fellow was yelling, 'I'm shot! I'm shot!' And I said, 'Well, die, you son of a bitch! Die!' We didn't have film to waste on that.

How did you become a producer for Paramount?

After the war my brother and I rented a house in Hollywood, and there was a little red-cheeked Jewish boy, very bright guy. I used to talk stories with him. I really didn't know quite what he did. It was Irving Thalberg, who was the [production] head of Metro-Goldwyn. He was the great genius in the picture business. One day out of a clear sky, Jesse Lasky called me and asked me to come up and see him. He asked if I would like to take charge of making forty pictures for him. I said, 'You must be nuts.' He said, 'No, Thalberg says you know more about stories than anybody else that he knows, so I'd like to have you.' I said, 'Is he the little fellow – ?' He said, 'Yeah.' I said, 'What does he do?' He said, 'He's in charge of Metro-Goldwyn. Anyway, I'd like to know, in the next two months, forty pictures that we're going to make. You have got to get the stories and who's gonna be in 'em and the directors. You think you can do it?' I said, 'How much money do I have to do it with?' He said, 'All you want.' I said, 'Sure, I can do it.' At that time, all stories for pictures were written just for pictures, and the writers weren't too hot. But I went out and bought two Zane Greys, two Joseph Conrads, two Rex Beaches, two Jack Londons – you name it, I bought 'em. Anybody could buy 'em; nobody had ever sold anything. We could buy a story for $5,000 to $15,000. It was a windfall for them. Nobody got rich being an author in those days. In two weeks' time, I had forty pictures and had 'em cast. Then all I had to do was to get the people to write 'em. That was the most successful year Paramount ever had. I remember one time in the 1920s when Jack Ford and I were talking with some executive, and the executive said, 'Christ, Howard, how come you know so much about stories?' And Jack Ford said, 'He reads books.' I really had too much to do at Paramount, because I was writing the titles – they were silent pictures – and reading the scripts and seeing the rushes. I got tired after about six months, so I hired some newspapermen to write titles, and they became big guns. I started the horrible thing of associate producers. But I wrote titles till I was blue in the face. If you didn't like a story, you could change it just by writing different

4 Leatrice Joy in *The Dressmaker from Paris*.

titles. There was one picture [*Lucretia Lombard*, 1923] that had Irene Rich and Norma Shearer. I liked Norma Shearer, and I didn't think much of Irene Rich, so I made Norma the heroine and reversed the whole thing. The director [Jack Conway] was very pleased with it.

You were given screen credit I think four times for scripts or stories you did for features before you became a director – Quicksands, Tiger Love [*1924*], The Dressmaker from Paris [*1925*], *and* Honesty – The Best Policy [*1926*]. *Were those the only four?*
Probably. I didn't write *Dressmaker from Paris*. I just thought of the title and gave a writer [Adelaide Heilbron] the idea for a story, and she wrote it. Paul Bern directed that. He was a talented guy.

What about Tiger Love?
I don't remember that. That's a long time to remember.

Do you remember Honesty – The Best Policy?
No. I have a hunch that some of those things were suggestions and that they just credit me with them. I never even saw the pictures.

You made Victor Fleming a director, didn't you, when he was just a cameraman?
He was very capable, and I had a good deal of confidence in him. He was a good cameraman, so I knew that things were gonna come in that way pretty good. He made a very good picture one time [*Empty Hands*, 1924], a rather delicate little picture, and the first few days he got all tied up and asked me to come down. He said, 'How the hell am I gonna tell people to do this kind of stuff?' You know, he was tough. The girl was Norma Shearer. She was fabulous. I wanted to sign her for Paramount. Lasky saw her and he said, 'She's bowlegged and she's got a cast in one eye. Did you fall for her or something like that?' I said, 'No, I didn't fall for her, I just think she's good.' When he saw the picture he damn near broke both legs trying to get out and sign her up. In the meantime I'd shown it to Irving Thalberg and Thalberg signed her [he also married her; Hawks became Thalberg's brother-in-law in 1928 by marrying Shearer's

sister Athole]. Fleming made a very good picture, but he needed a little help with the method of acting. You see, in those days scenes were overplayed. And I started to underwrite. Vic at this time thought that I'd written some emotional scenes for him to do, and when I showed him what it was, it was easy.

You worked with Ben Hecht on the script of Underworld [1927].
Ben Hecht sold a story to me. Ben and I worked on the story, and a friend [Art Rosson] was to be the director. He went up to San Francisco, as I remember, to go to the prison there, but unfortunately got tight, so they had to fire him. We had sketches made of every scene. We had sets built, and we had a cast. It was beautifully written. Then we got Joe Von Sternberg to direct the picture, and out came this really good picture. So no matter how he acted towards other people, he was always very nice to me. Louis B. Mayer one time thought that by hiring Von Sternberg and I as directors, he would make a doubly good picture. The moment we left his office I laughed about it, I said, 'Joe, that's the silliest thing I've ever known. I couldn't keep a straight face in there.' He said, 'Me either.' Because I take a great big situation and play it way down, and he takes a little situation and plays it way up. 'Well,' I said, 'for fun, let's prepare a story. Then let's go in and tell him your way of doing it and my way of doing it, and see which one he wants.' So we got up to a certain point, we laid the story out, and then instead of doing a treatment or anything we went in and told it. They took my way of doing it and turned Joe down.

Hecht said in his autobiography that he was upset about what Sternberg did to the script of Underworld. *He said Sternberg added 'sentimental' things to it.*
I think it was a damned good film. Hecht kind of would resent somebody and find something to say about him. I got along with him, but I know that was a habit of his. And I think probably Joe's arrogance got to him.

You said once that Ernst Lubitsch was one of your three favourite directors [the other two were John Ford and Leo McCarey]. Which

5 *Underworld*: Clive Brook.

of Lubitsch's films did you study most when you were starting out? I studied them all. He was at Paramount when I was there. We became very good friends. I liked – what was it? I can't remember names – the one where Emil Jannings was a czar and ran around from his mistress and kept running through doors [*The Patriot*, 1928]. And I thought the musical that he made with the 'Beyond the Blue Horizon' song in it [*Monte Carlo*, 1930] was great. Oh, some of those things were just lovely. He was quite a character. When he saw *Sergeant York*, he said, 'Howard, how can any man in his right mind make two or three reels of a picture about a man shooting a gun?' I said, 'I don't know, Ernst. How the hell can a man in his right mind make two or three reels of people coming in and out of doorways?'

You left Paramount in 1924 and went to MGM's story department. After I'd produced about sixty pictures, Thalberg said, 'Well, now you've had a beginning. Now come over and do the same thing at Metro.' I said, 'I want to direct.' He said, 'Do this for one year and then you can direct.' Then at the end of a year I said, 'A year ago you said I could direct. You fooled me.' He said, 'Howard, Christ, we can get all the directors we need. I can't get anybody to do your work.' I said, 'I just quit this morning.' He and I were very good friends, and he said, 'Nothing could change your mind?' I said, 'Nothing can change it.' 'Well,' he said, 'I could let you direct.' I said, 'No, I don't want you to do that. You can let me direct some time after I show you what I can do.' And I went off to play golf. I ran into the head of Fox Studios [Sol M. Wurtzel]. He said, 'What are you doing?' I said, 'Playing golf.' 'No,' he said, 'I mean where you working?' I said, 'Playing golf.' 'Aren't you working at Metro?' I said no. He said, 'Well, then you started at Fox this morning.' I said, 'No, I had enough of that job. I'm gonna direct.' He said, 'OK, you started to direct.' I said, 'What do you want me to direct?' He said, 'Write your own story.' And so I started directing.

Your first feature as a director, The Road to Glory [*1926*], *apparently doesn't exist. I read the plot synopsis, and it seems a very solemn thing, quite unlike the films you did later.*

15

It was taken from a little incident that happened once where a beautiful girl went blind from drinking bootleg liquor at my house. While we were waiting for the doctor, she said, 'Just because I'm blind it doesn't mean I can't perform pretty good in bed.' Nobody seemed interested in that kind of thing then. I loved the attitude that she had, and I wrote the story which was a very dramatic, serious, downbeat story. It didn't have any fun in it. It was pretty bad. I don't think anybody enjoyed it except for a few critics. And Wurtzel, who was a very astute and wise man, said, 'Look, you've shown you can make a picture, but for God's sake, go out and make entertainment.' So I went home and wrote a story that night about Adam and Eve waking up in the Garden of Eden and called it *Fig Leaves*. It got its cost back in one theatre. And that taught me a very good lesson; from that time on, I've been following his advice about trying to make entertainment.

Part of it was supposed to have been in colour.
I couldn't remember *Fig Leaves* until I saw it a couple of years ago in France. I thought it was amazingly modern. It's got two reels of colour in it. I didn't know how to use colour, so I got this big set, had it done in black and silver, had all the colour taken out of it. And if I remember right, I don't think the colour showed up. I think they printed that part in black-and-white. The story starts in the Garden of Eden and becomes modern. About the only strange thing about it was how we got from old-time to modern. It was the days when they didn't have a laboratory to make dissolves, so a very fine cameraman [Joseph August] and I got together, and we tried to get something a little different. We wanted it to get all fuzzy and then dissolve to the new thing. And the way we did it was to get a beer bottle that had a flaw in it and put it in front of the lens. We turned it from the clear place to the place where the flaw began to show up. But we had an awful time, because somebody lost the beer bottle, so we never could get back from the new stuff to the old in the end of the picture.

What do you remember about another of your early pictures at Fox, Fazil?
Christ Almighty, can you imagine Charlie Farrell as an Arabian

6 *A Girl in Every Port*: Louise Brooks.

7 *A Girl in Every Port*: a typical Hawks situation of two male friends and a girl – Robert Armstrong, Victor McLaglen and Louise Brooks.

8 *The Air Circus*: Two male friends and a girl amidst the camaraderie of the group.

sheikh? Charlie was such a shy, withdrawn guy, and we had a beautiful Swedish girl, Greta Nissen, in it. Their courtship ended by drawing back from a shot of the Eiffel Tower down to the two of them in bed under a sheet. I told the girl, 'Now, Charlie's real shy, you're going to have to do something under those covers.' And I told Charlie, 'Now, this girl's real shy . . .' Well, they were two of the busiest beavers you've ever seen in all your life. At least I got fun out of *that*.

The Air Circus?
Air Circus was a good picture. It was about two kids learning to fly, and they took off and flew in the picture: they actually soloed. The only trouble was at that time sound came in, and they asked me, 'What do you know about dialogue?' And I said, 'I just know how people speak.' So they gave me a dialogue director [Lewis R. Seiler] who used to be a burlesque comic for Minsky's. He made the dialogue scenes because I wouldn't make them. I said, 'Nobody talks like that.' Seiler was a director who did anything they wanted him to do. And you have never *known* such bad dialogue. So I

didn't make a picture for a year and a half. They wanted everybody to make a scene to show that they could use dialogue. We all had a hell of a time. And the production head, Winnie Sheehan, didn't like me because I made a picture called *A Girl in Every Port* where we threw a cop into the water. Sheehan used to be a police commissioner in New York, and he didn't like to see that. When he came out of the preview, he said, 'This is the worst picture that Fox ever made.' It got its cost back in one theatre. So he didn't like me too well. And every time I got a story ready, he'd turn it down.

Why was your last silent picture, Trent's Last Case, *not made as a talkie?*
That was one of the great detective stories of all time. The only trouble was we had Raymond Griffith as the star and he talked like this [in a hoarse whisper due to damaged vocal cords]. We had it all written for dialogue because I thought it would be cute to have him say, 'Now I want you to do this . . .' The day we'd started shooting, they said, 'It's got to be a silent picture. We can't have him talking like this.' The picture never showed anywhere [except in England]. We turned it into a gag comedy.

4

Talking Pictures

How did you feel about sound films when you started making them?
I thought it was so easy.

I have a feeling you were one of the few directors who probably welcomed the transition. You and John Ford really set the style of acting in films in the sound era because the two of you quickly grasped the idea that broad stage acting would never work for sound.
I think you're pretty smart to recognize it, because Ford and I said, 'They talk too much,' and we cut down the dialogue on every scene we made. We cut lines out because actors just loved it when they got a whole bunch of lines. And Ford and I didn't think they were good. Also, when you leave the dialogue out and make visual stuff, the visual stuff has so much more impact because you hadn't used it before. When I was making *The Dawn Patrol* [1930], which was my first talking picture, I got forty letters from the front office [First National] saying that I'd missed chances of doing good scenes because I'd underdone them so much. I've saved the letters just for fun. The dialogue before that reminded you of a villain talking on a riverboat, *Uncle Tom's Cabin* or something like that. They hammed it up. And I stopped them from doing that in *Dawn Patrol*. They weren't used to normal dialogue. They weren't used to normal reading. They wanted to have somebody beat his chest and wave his arms. But when Thalberg saw the picture, he said, 'You son of a bitch. Everybody'll be trying to do that, and they won't know how to do it, and we'll get into more goddam trouble.' It was the biggest-grossing picture of the year. And then they decided I knew dialogue.

9 *The Dawn Patrol*: Richard Barthelmess, Douglas Fairbanks Jr, and Neil Hamilton.

In fact, they began showing it to other directors and saying, 'That's the kind of dialogue we want.' It was used as an example for years.
After that it was easy. Nobody asked me if I knew it. It was just a new form of acting, and that doesn't happen very much. People liked the scenes because they were underdone, because they were thrown away. Nobody emoted in the pictures that I made. Then the funny thing was Kazan came along and started going back to the old scream and holler days.

Nowadays a lot of movies go to the opposite extreme. There's no emotion in a lot of them. It's very cool.
I've never gone *that* far. In the first place, you have to write pretty

21

good to do it, or else it isn't gonna mean anything. It's just gonna sit there. Then you've got some actors nowadays who are very popular, like Eastwood, Burt Reynolds – Christ, nothing could make *them* emote. Nobody was ever cooler than Bacall. She couldn't emote if her life depended on it. She just had a good grin, and she could say a line, and that was it. See, if you try to keep up high all the time, you're just gonna tire 'em out. And you're gonna annoy 'em, because nobody is capable of writing in such a fashion that you can keep emotion at a high pitch all the time.

The Dawn Patrol *has been called an antiwar film.*
Well, it wasn't done purposely. I've never made a picture to be anti anything or pro anything. I flew, I knew what the Air Force was up against. I used that theme from *Dawn Patrol* in another picture about war, and the theme is very simple. It's a man who's in command and sends people out to die and then he's killed himself and some other poor bastard has to send them out to die. It's the same theme in *The Road to Glory* [1936], a picture that Faulkner wrote, only one was in the trenches and one was in the air.

10 *The Road To Glory* (1936): A girl and two men – June Lang with
Fredric March . . .

11 . . . and Warner Baxter.

5

The Business of Movies

You have a reputation as one of the most astute businessmen of all directors. You've never been tied for a long time to any studio, and you've always maintained a high degree of control over your work. The producing aspect of your career is very important because you only exercise creative control by controlling the money.

I've been independent except for two or three pictures in the first couple years. It's very easy to figure out that I didn't have much to do with 'em. I've been independent ever since that time. And I started a lot of trouble by saying 'Directed by Howard Hawks' and 'Produced' afterward, making the direction more important. A lot of producers didn't like that.

How much correlation is there between how much you like a film personally and how well it does commercially?

I hate to say this, but I don't think any of them that I didn't like did any good. I made those films trying to do favours for people who I liked very much. I'd say, 'I don't know how to make that kind of a goddam film.' They'd say, 'Oh, yes, you do,' and I'd make it, and it wasn't any good. I won't say what pictures they were.

How much control do you have over the editing of your films?

Oh, practically complete control. I've had a little trouble on a couple of pictures that they thought were too long. I made the mistake of making them too long, and they made the mistake of trying to shorten them.

Since you also produce your own pictures, do you find that you have to worry much about money matters during production?

It all depends. For fifteen or twenty years, I've worked on the profits of my pictures, not working for a company, so I'm damned interested in how much they cost and how much they gross. But I don't think it has any effect at all. I think you're out to do as well as you can, but you're not about to throw money away. If you do, you find yourself pretty soon without a picture.

What are the differences you find in the economics of film-making and distribution between today and the past?
There isn't any comparison. In the 1920s I made *Fig Leaves*, and it got its cost back in one theatre. And that was at about ten cents admission or twenty cents admission. Nowadays – oh, we made a picture up in Idaho, every Indian pony cost us $86 a day to work with. You could have gone up there and rented the pony for fifty cents. And they'd have been happy to have rented it to you. It's almost impossible to make a picture around here. The shooting schedule of *El Dorado* [1967] was at least twice as long as on *Rio Bravo* [1959], which was made in the same location, practically the same cast. The prices in making a picture went up so that it cost us three times as much to make *El Dorado* as it did to make *Rio Bravo*. The last movie, the last western [*Rio Lobo*, 1970], cost $1,000,000 less by going down to Mexico than it would cost here. Used the same people, the same sets, same film, same everything. Just didn't have the unions to combat. If anything's the matter, it's the unions. We had a little two-sided shack to put up for *El Dorado*. Cost $14,000 to build it. In the 1920s they'd have put it up for $250. As a matter of fact, you wouldn't have gotten a gang, you'd just ask the one grip to put it up, and he had it up in two hours.

Today a film-maker has to spend two years making the deal and then, after he makes a film, another year supervising the contracts and the foreign versions. Do you feel that has hurt the industry?
I don't think they're doing anything right in the whole industry at the present time. Some agents are trying to make more money than the director or the writers and everything. There's nothing you can do about it unless you get in there and go through it, right from top to bottom. And that's an awful job.

Do you believe in previewing, especially in the case of comedies? Do
you get audience response and then cut the film accordingly?
Not too much. I'm not too great a believer in previews, but
sometimes they're good. Sometimes they tell you a lot. When we
previewed *To Have and Have Not*, we had a new girl [Lauren
Bacall], and she was different. I was a little worried about her, about
whether the audience would like her, if they would laugh. She had
one line in the beginning of the thing, so I waited until they laughed
like hell, and then I went out and got a couple of drinks. I came back
in and Jack Warner said, 'Where the hell have you been?' I said,
'Out having some drinks. How's it going?' He said, 'Just great. Why
did you leave?' I said, 'I knew when they laughed at that thing, they
were going to laugh at her all the way through.' You can find out
whether you've got a funny character. The first time I used Walter
Brennan [in *Barbary Coast*] I was quite worried about him, whether
he was going to be funny. I never worried after the first time. We
took the picture out one night to preview it. Nobody laughed at all.
The audience just sat there. I came out rather stunned and looked up
to see what picture was playing, and it was Will Rogers; he was
killed that afternoon [August 15, 1935]. But for about half an hour,
I didn't know what had happened. We took the picture out the next
night, and people laughed and roared. That was the most frustrating
thing that ever happened to me. If you make a comedy, you take it
out and the people laugh, you're *immediately* pleased, you get an
immediate reaction and the pleasure that you've done a good job. If
you make a drama, it takes a little bit longer. You have to have
people come up to you and say, 'I enjoyed that,' because they can
give you no visible expression in a theatre. Oh, if they don't walk
out, that's pretty good. I think probably the last picture that worked
out well is your favourite for a while, and then you start thinking
about it, and you go back a little further. Not that you're trying to
make every scene a great scene, but you try not to annoy the
audience. I told John Wayne when we started to work together,
'Duke, if you can make three good scenes in this picture and don't
annoy the audience the rest of the time, you'll be good.' He said, 'Do
you believe that?' I said, 'Yeah. If I make five good scenes in this
picture, and don't annoy the audience, I think I'll be good.' So he

started to work on that. And he always comes up to me and says, 'Hey, is this one of those scenes?' I'd say, 'This is the one where you get it over just as quickly as you can and don't annoy the audience.' 'OK.' We work that way, and now he preaches that as though it's gospel, and he does a great job of not annoying the audience. As we got to be better friends working together, I could hear him telling some actor who was trying to ham it up, 'Look, the boss says this. You see that you do it. Get it over in a hurry. This is one of those scenes.' I never realized that he was playing policeman for me on the last two or three pictures.

Some people feel that a comedy should run only about ninety minutes. Do you think there's a particular rule about running time when it comes to comedy?
I think it would be a good idea to keep those people from expressing their ideas. They don't know what the hell it's all about. I made a picture called *Man's Favorite Sport?* Universal got the best preview cards that they'd ever gotten on a picture. They got so damned excited that they said, 'Look, now, if you'll take forty minutes out of it, you can get in another show in a day.' They gave me a list of things, and I said, 'What is that?' 'The things that you could take out.' And I said, 'Well, I think that it's a list of the things that have to stay *in.*' So they cut twenty minutes out of it, took it out and previewed it, and the cards weren't nearly as good. They cut twenty minutes more out of it and previewed it, and the cards were lousy, and some people walked out on it, and they released it that way.

What ever inspires them to such decision-making?
Don't ask me! I had a picture called *The Big Sky*, and they asked me to fly back to Chicago. I said, 'What do you want me to do back there?' 'We want you to see the lines – they go clear around the corner trying to get in to see the picture. Now, if you take footage out of it, we could get another show in.' I said, 'The trouble is I don't know what you could take out.' Because ordinarily I take out more stuff than they want. Well, they took some stuff out, and next week they didn't have any lines at all.

27

They left it that way?
Yeah. Producers like that are stupid people. They're just really stupid.

6

Working with Writers: I

Most of your movies, even the oldest ones, look very fresh and modern today. Why do you think that is?
Most of them were well written. That's why they last. I've always been blessed with great writers. As a matter of fact, I'm such a coward that unless I get a great writer, I don't want to make a picture. But Hemingway, Faulkner, Hecht and MacArthur, Jules Furthman, all those people were damned good. The only time I tried to take somebody that I didn't know was good, why, I had to do it over again. So I've been very lucky getting good writers, and I think that they make an awful lot of difference in the picture.

How much writing do you do on your own pictures?
Well, I think that if you see the pictures that I make, you'll find a certain similarity in the dialogue and the fact that it's short and quick and rather hard. I practically always work in a room with the writers.

Why do you so rarely take a writing credit on screen?
Because if I did, I couldn't get such good writers to work with me.

Could you explain how the day-to-day writing goes on a script? Were you all together in a room batting it out on a typewriter?
I can't play the typewriter. I couldn't write anything *per se*. I mean, I couldn't write a book or do anything like that. When Hecht and MacArthur and I used to work on a script, we'd get started around 7:30 in the morning, and we'd work for two hours, and then we'd play backgammon for an hour. Then we'd start again, and one of us would be one character, and one would be another character. We'd read our lines of dialogue, and the whole idea was to try and stump

the other people, to see if they could think of something crazier than you could. That is the kind of dialogue we used, and the kind that was fun. We could usually remember what we said, and put it right down and go on working. And sometimes you're so far in a picture, and you get an idea that you're going to change a character, so you just go back and change the lines that you've written for that character, and start all over again. Hecht and MacArthur were just marvellous. The first picture we worked on they said, 'Oh, we're all through now.' I said, 'No, tomorrow we start on something new.' The fellows said, 'What?' I said, 'Different ways of saying things.' And they had more fun, we had more fun, for about three days saying things in different ways. I'd say, 'How do you say this – you've got a line, "Oh, you're just in love".' One of them came up with, 'Oh, you're just broke out in monkey bites.' The audience knows vaguely what you're saying, they like the method of saying it. We go through the entire script in sequence; one of us suggests something, and what you suggest somebody else twists around. I learned it from Hemingway. Noël Coward came to see me once when I was over at Columbia, introduced himself, and said, 'What do you call the kind of dialogue that you use?' And I said, 'Well, Hemingway calls it oblique dialogue. I call it three-cushion. Because you hit it over here and over here and go over here to get the meaning. You don't state it right out.' We discussed it for quite a while. Another time Capra and I spent a couple of hours talking about it, and he went off and made I think the finest example of that kind of dialogue. Jean Arthur was in love with Jimmy Stewart [in *Mr Smith Goes to Washington*], and she was trying to persuade Thomas Mitchell to marry her because she was in love with Stewart. That was oblique if there ever was one. We talked it over until he got the line, then he went and did it better than I did. I believe that this particular method makes the audience do the work rather than coming out and making a kind of stupid scene out of it.

Plots tend to be more important in films than characters. Quite often the characters behave according to the dictates of the plot. But you usually did it the other way around.
There's a very simple theory behind that. There are about thirty

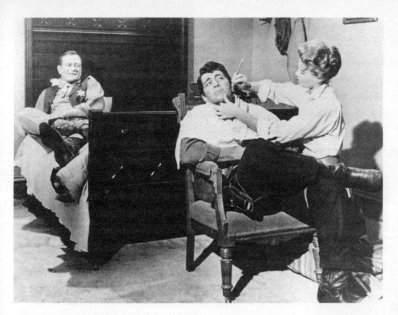

12 *Rio Bravo*: Watching an old friend get rehabilitated – John Wayne, Dean Martin and Angie Dickinson.

plots in all of drama. They've all been done by very good people. If you can think of a new way to tell that plot, you're pretty good. But if you can do characters, you can forget about the plot. You just have the characters moving around. Let them tell the story for you, and don't worry about the plot. I don't. Movements come from characterization. A lot of the things in *Rio Bravo* happened because Wayne was watching an old friend get rehabilitated. And then just when Dean Martin started to come out of all this trouble and get better, he got caught while he was taking a bath. Because somebody said 'You stink' to him. I like that kind of storytelling. And if you'll notice, almost all the men in my pictures have gone through some troubles. Then they have to be straightened out. That makes interesting writing.

Hemingway said that the best storytelling is like an iceberg – only one-eighth of it is above the water, the rest is down below.
Yeah. If a girl is gonna say how broke she was, you've got to find an

awful good metaphor to use, you know. Something that happened, that's how broke she was. You make a picture, you draw a picture of it. See, if you're gonna do something, do it with characters. Do 'em a little differently. Every scene's been done. Now, your job is to do 'em a little differently. To get mad a little differently. To steal a little differently.

Are there scenes in your films you look back at and you think, 'Oh, that's flat, I should have done it differently'?
Sure. That's why I steal it and do it again.

Are there books you've wanted to make into movies but haven't been able to buy?
Oh, Lord, I've tried to buy lots of stories that I haven't gotten. I wanted to do the Bond series. It was done by my former assistant director Cubby Broccoli.

What was it about the Bond books that appealed to you?
The great imagination that the writer [Ian Fleming] had. As far as stories go, if I like a story, I make it. Not always – I buy three stories and throw one away, or maybe two out of the three, after I work on them. I don't have to throw 'em away, I can usually sell 'em to some poor guy who doesn't know enough. But if you get a good story, it's easy to make, and if you get a bad story, you have an awful time.

I wonder why you never made a film of the Maxwell Anderson–Laurence Stallings play What Price Glory? *It's almost like one of your stories.*
Too much like 'em! There's no doubt that I've been influenced by *What Price Glory?* It was a really good play, and it was beautifully done as a picture by Raoul Walsh.

How do you come up with names for characters?
By just thinking of people. Wayne said to me [on *Rio Bravo*], 'Hey, that's a good name you've got for me – Chance.' And I said, 'Well, she was a damn good-looking girl.' In *His Girl Friday*, we had a fellow called Stairway Sam. He was always watching girls' legs go

up and down a flight of stairs. That came after we finished the script. Another thing was when Cary Grant said to this gorilla, 'There's a guy down in the car waiting,' and he said, 'What does he look like?' Well, they had a description of him. I said, 'That's kind of dull.' Ben Hecht said, 'I know what he could say – "He looks like the actor Ralph Bellamy [who was playing the part]."' Now a line like *that* you could remember. That got a big laugh.

You're fond of giving your characters nicknames. Does Bogart call Bacall 'Slim' in To Have and Have Not, *even though the character's name is Marie, because you called your wife* [Nancy Gross, Hawks's second wife] *'Slim'?*
Yes.

And why does Bacall call Bogart 'Steve', even though his character's name is Harry?
Because my wife called me Steve.

Didn't you once say that Victor Fleming and you used to call each other 'Dan'? Why was that?
Well, I think we just started. He'd say, 'Dan, what are you gonna do?' And I'd say, 'Dan, I don't know.' And we'd go out and get into some kind of trouble.

You like to rewrite dialogue on the set, don't you?
Because if I don't write big, nobody can read my writing. No, but actually, if I got an actor who was particularly good and had a certain quirk or something he did that I liked, I'd rewrite the part for him. It makes it a lot easier. You're not really rewriting it, you're just saying it in different words, with a different attitude. When we started *Tiger Shark*, Eddie Robinson's character was written as a very dour, sour man. At the end of the first day I said to Eddie, 'This is going to be the dullest picture that's ever been made.' And he said, 'What can we do?' I said, 'Well, if you're willing to try it with me, why, let's make him a happy-go-lucky, talkative . . . you're going to have to keep talking all through the picture.' He said, 'Fine, let's do it.' So every day I gave him a sheet of yellow paper and said, 'Here's

your lines.' He's a fine actor, and I thought he did a great job. But I hate to think of what the picture would have been if we'd done the dour, sour man instead of this rather gay, futile man, because the whole tenor of the picture changed. They talk about 'improvisation'. That's one of the silliest words that's used in the motion picture industry. What the hell do they think a director *does*? How do you expect that we can go out with a story that's written up in a room, go out to the location, and do it verbatim? I have never found a writer who could imagine a thing so that you can do it like that. And somebody started saying it's 'improvising'. Well, I wish you could see some pictures that are *not* improvised – where they send them out and say, 'We don't want you to change a word or a scene or anything.' We have a scene that we're going to do: I'm interested first in the action and next in the words they speak. If I can't make the action good, I don't use the words. If I want something to happen in a hurry, I can't have a man stop and read a line coming in. I let him run on through yelling something. I must change to fit the action because, after all, it's a motion picture. Some of the stuff that's handed to you on paper is perfectly good to read, but it isn't any good on the set. [Hawks on another occasion put this point even more forcefully, telling me, 'If it reads good, it won't play good.']

Leo McCarey, whom you regarded highly, was one of the loosest of all Hollywood directors. He would literally make up whole scenes on the set. How do you feel he managed to do that?
You say 'one of the loosest' – I think *all* the good ones are loose. None of them made a scene until they thought it was any good. I watched Leo McCarey sit on a set all morning and never do a scene. Then he'd do four hours' work in the afternoon. Directors are storytellers. If we can't change something, we're no good. Because you're not trying to photograph a budget or a cost sheet. You're trying to make a scene that's going to be good, the best you know how. If you don't, it's your own damn fault.

7

Working with Actors

What I love most about your films is the feeling you get of people behaving spontaneously toward each other. And it's maybe the theme of your work, the importance of relationships. It comes across in the sense you get of actors working on the set together. For example, there's a scene at the end of El Dorado *when Wayne puts the crutch under his arm, and Mitchum says, 'You've got it under the wrong arm!' And Wayne says, 'How would you know? You've been using it first under this arm and then the other!' I assume that was a joke that was carried over into the film from the actors kidding each other on the set.*

Well, we'd all forgotten which side he got shot on. So I had to do something about it. Actually it doesn't mean a damn thing, it just was the temperament of two guys and what they did to one another.

There are a lot of scenes like that in your films. You get the feeling of a group of people really relating to each other, and not just reading lines on a page.

Any time you get somebody who's as good as Wayne and Mitchum, you're going to make better scenes than there are in the script. Because they're damn good, those two people are together. And it's always easy to make a picture with Wayne if you've got somebody good for him to buck up against. Otherwise he blows 'em right off the screen, and you don't get anything. In *Red River* he had Montgomery Clift; in *Rio Bravo* he had Dean Martin; and in this one you had Mitchum. Those people are good. You don't blow *them* off. And they're not trying to outdo one another or anything. They'll do anything you ask 'em to do. Mitchum started out to give me his idea of playing a drunk, and I said, 'Hell, Dean Martin did that in the last picture. Can't we find another way of doing a

35

13 *El Dorado*: 'Any time you get somebody who's as good as Wayne and Mitchum, you're going to make better scenes than there are in the script.'

drunk?' So we did. And we had a lot more fun in that picture. I mean, I think some of the reactions are much funnier. But I'll tell you, when you get two people who are good, it's pretty easy to do this kind of stuff. And I think the story had it. Any time you get a story where one man takes care of another and shows that he's fond of him and will go through all of the things that happen – the relationship between Bogart and Brennan in *To Have and Have Not* was such a great relationship – a man with a drunk. That was expressed in one line. The fellow who rented their boat said, 'What do you take care of him for?' Bogart looked at him and said, 'He thinks he's taking care of *me*.' And he wasn't very nice the way he said it. Those are the relationships that happen between men. You begin to get that feeling, and then you read things into the scenes. For instance, the relationship between Wayne and Dean Martin in *Rio Bravo* worked out best with Martin trying to roll a cigarette and Wayne watching him and rolling it for him because Martin's fingers were shaking. Then because that worked good, why, we did it a couple of more times in the picture.

Wayne did a scene like that in True Grit. *He's rolling a cigarette, and the girl takes it from him and says, 'Here, let me do that for you.'*
Wayne remembers pretty good. If the thing is good, why, he tries it again. More power to him.

What is the reason for the running bit of business in A Girl in Every Port *of one guy pulling the other guy's finger?*
You ever hit anybody hard? Your finger goes out of joint, and somebody takes it and pulls it back into joint. I hit Hemingway, and I broke the whole back of my hand. I wish it had just gone out of joint.

Why did you hit Hemingway?
He just said, 'Can you hit?' I broke my whole hand. He laughed like hell, and he sat up all night making a splint out of a tomato can so that I could go shooting with him the next morning. It didn't do my hand any good. It's an absolutely different shape.

37

Was the finger business in A Girl in Every Port *supposed to be a gesture of friendship? You used it again with Kirk Douglas and Dewey Martin in* The Big Sky.

Oh, it's just like Wayne rolling cigarettes for Dean Martin. One thing you can do is look at all the pictures I've ever made, and you'll see that nobody pats another person on the back. That's the goddamnedest inane thing I've ever known.

How do you rehearse actors?

Part of it is if I'd think of something, I'd go to the actor and say, 'Don't tell this other guy about it, but read such-and-such a line.' He throws the line to the other actor, and the other actor at first doesn't know what to say, and then he responds in his own way, and it always works out well. You don't have to do a lot of rehearsing with any good actor. You merely tell them what you're trying to get out of a scene, then you just turn them loose and let them go.

In Rio Bravo, *when Walter Brennan mimics John Wayne at one point, did Dean Martin know it was coming? There's something about the way Martin looks that makes me think it was a complete surprise to him.*

If I answer yes, I'll have at least a fifty percent chance of being right, because I don't do scenes twice if I can help it. Did you see the George Plimpton show [*Shootout at Rio Lobo*, a 1970 TV documentary about Hawks at work]? It typifies the way we work more than anything else that's ever been made. I told John Wayne to show Plimpton how to walk the way he does. But I didn't tell him to go through that marvellous routine that he went through. That was almost all ad-lib, as it were. I told him what to do, but he did it much better than I told him. And I told the rest of the actors the dumbest thing in the world is an actor getting serious about himself. For God's sake, don't get so serious about it.

That reminds me of something funny that happened on the Academy Awards show when you received your Oscar. Wayne presented it to you after making a crack about how he 'directed' you onto the stage for the award, but then when the two of you walked

off, Wayne started to leave the stage in the wrong direction, and you had to motion him which way to go. Was that an accident?
No. I said, 'Duke, go off the wrong way and I'll stop you.'

How do you keep the atmosphere from getting too serious on the set when the cameras start to roll?
Instead of saying 'Action!', which I think is a silly way to start a scene, I say 'Camera.' Because if you're gonna do a quiet scene and you say 'Action!' – oh, God, you should have seen some of the early directors, some of the silent directors over at Fox. There was one fellow who used to stand right under the camera, and he'd crouch as though he was going to spring at 'em. And he'd say, 'Now is everybody ready? Are you ready? All right! *Number One!*' And then in the middle of the scene he'd say, '*Number Two! Three and Four!*'

When you're doing comedy, take after take after take, how do you keep it fresh?
I don't *let* them do take after take after take. If a person isn't good enough to do it, I just have somebody else walk in, or else I forget that scene and start on something else. I don't go back to it. I don't believe in getting myself tired out along with the actors. You just try and make a funny picture. If it isn't funny, you drop the thing. I think that when actors get to mumbling over lines so long, they get very bad, but if they just come out with it, they usually say the right thing. Brando started out as a great actor. I had a talk with him when he made a picture called *One-Eyed Jacks.* Paramount asked me if I could do anything to make it better, because they lost their shirt on it. He said, 'Did you like it?' And I said, 'No.' He said, 'Don't you think I'm a good actor?' I said, 'You take much too long to do a scene.' He slowed up until he got so dull that it drove me nuts, I couldn't stand watching him. But if you've got a good scene, you can let an actor stall and play with it. If it isn't a good scene, the quicker you get it over with the better you are. I work at about twenty percent faster speed than the average picture. When an actor does a scene, I say, 'Do it in twenty seconds less and it'll be pretty good.' And if they *don't* do it in twenty seconds less, then I cut it down to practically nothing and tell them to go ahead with it.

Because it's just as good a scene, and it gets it over in a hurry. Actors get all confused. They stall in making scenes. It takes you a couple of days to get with them. They don't like to hop on somebody's lines. I would say, 'If you *don't* hop on the line, I'll throw you out of here.' So they hop on the line. The old school as far as theatre goes is, 'Don't speak over somebody's lines.' I *want* them to speak over the lines. I want the sound man to tell me whether or not he can understand. If he can understand, that's fine.

It occurs to me that you are so much like some of the characters in your films. You have that same laconic wit.
I think I'm probably the worst actor that's ever been in a film. The first time I tried to do it, I stumbled and fell down. I can't remember a line.

It's sometimes said that a director can bludgeon an actor into giving a good performance.
I don't think that's true.

But on the other hand, Dean Martin, for example, is an actor who's never really distinguished himself except in Rio Bravo. *It was a fantastic performance. There are a few other films where he's pretty good, but not as good as he was for you. How did you get that performance out of him?*
You have to have good people to play a drunk. Because you could get some people to play a drunk and it nauseates you. Dean Martin was pretty good, but people didn't give him enough help in doing it. He could do anything you wanted him to. I hired him because an agent wanted me to meet him. And I said, 'Well, get him around here at nine o'clock tomorrow morning.' The agent said, 'He can't be here at nine.' So he came in about 10:30, and I said, 'Why the hell couldn't you be here at nine o'clock?' He said, 'I was working in Las Vegas, and I had to hire an airplane and fly down here.' And that made me think, 'Well, my Lord, this guy really wants to work.' So I said, 'You'd better go over and get some wardrobe.' He said, 'Am I hired?' And I said, 'Yeah. Anybody who'll do that ought to get a chance to do it.' He came back from wardrobe looking like a

musical comedy cowboy. I said, 'Dean, look, you know a little about drinking. You've seen a lot of drunks. I want a *drunk*. I want a guy in an old dirty sweatshirt and an old hat.' And he said, 'OK, you don't have to tell me any more.' He went over, and he came back with the outfit that he wore in the picture. He must have been successful because Jack Warner said to me, 'We hired Dean Martin. When's he going to be in this picture?' I said, 'He's the funny-looking guy in the old hat.' 'Holy smoke, is that Dean Martin?' Dean did a great job. It was fun working with him. All you had to do was tell him something. The scene where he had a hangover, which he did in most of the scenes, there was one where he was suffering, and I said, 'Look, that's too damn polite. I knew a guy with a hangover who'd pound his leg trying to hurt himself to try and get some feeling in it.' 'OK, I know that kind of guy,' he said. 'I can do it.' And he went on and did the scene with no rehearsal or anything. Dean's a damn good actor, but he also is a fellow who floats through life. He has to be urged. He has to get some kind of a hint, something going, otherwise, hell, he won't even rehearse in some of his shows. He wants to get on and play golf.

I asked him about working with you and he said that you used to change the scenes every day so that they never could really learn their lines. They'd find out what they were gonna do when they came on the set. And he told me he was very worried because he had this big scene to do somewhere in the middle of the picture where he had to cry, or almost cry, and he was terrified of doing the scene and he hoped you'd never do it. He never said anything to you, and you put it off and never shot it until the very last day. He didn't know how you knew that, but he was very thankful to you that you didn't shoot it until the last day. And then you helped him through it, and it wasn't so hard.

Well, about that time I was willing to do almost anything, because he was so nice to work with and so good at what he did.

Is confidence what an actor needs most?
God knows what an actor needs. You have to find out what he needs and do it. When I've got a new girl, in starting a picture I get

14 *Only Angels Have Wings*: Cary Grant and Rita Hayworth.

eight members of the crew and say, 'Your line is this – when you run into her, you say this. When *you* run into her, you say this. When *you* run into her, you whistle.' By the time she gets ready to make a picture, she feels she's the Queen of Sheba. And all you have to do is be afraid of a relapse when she finds out how little she knows. The reason why stars are good, they walk in through a door and they think, 'Everybody wants to lay me.' Some poor little girl who's getting her first part, scared stiff, doesn't know what the hell to do. In making *Only Angels Have Wings*, Rita Hayworth was supposed to cry in one scene. Around eleven o'clock in the morning, I called an early lunch, and I changed the setting, put it outside, and brought in rain machines. She opened the door and played a scene, and rain hit her in the face. She was crying. All she had to do was to do that; her whole face was wet. She was supposed to play a drunk scene with Cary Grant, and I said, 'Cary, what's the matter with this thing?' He said, 'Howard, I don't know, she doesn't seem to know what I'm talking about.' So I sent the prop man for a big pitcher full of ice cubes and water, put it behind the bar, and told Rita to go in there and make a misstep and knock something off the bar. 'Cary,' I said, 'now, when you feel that the scene is dying, you just say, "You don't know what I'm talking about, do you?" and grab her by the neck and pour this whole thing right over her head. She'll holler or scream or do something, and we'll dissolve, and you put a towel over her head and be drying her hair and say, "What you want to know is this." You take her lines and your lines too.' She got quite a credit for playing a drunk scene and doing it well. But if we'd tried to make her *play* a drunk scene – when she finished the picture, Harry Cohn said to me, 'Anything you want – a boat or a racing car – it's yours. I got a new star.' I said, 'You *have* if you don't let her make a picture for six months. Bring people in and interview her. Ask her who's going to be the next president. Write about her. All this kind of thing. But don't put her in a picture until she builds up an ego.' And she sailed through the second picture. She never was a great actress, but she certainly was a beautiful girl. She had her ego built up so that she could play a scene.

8

Scarface and Howard Hughes

15 '*Scarface* is my favourite picture.'

Scarface is my favourite picture, even today, because we were completely alone, Hughes and I. Everybody was under contract to the studios. We couldn't get a studio, and they wouldn't loan us anybody, so we had to find a cast. They just didn't want independent pictures made in Hollywood. So we rented a little cobwebbed studio and opened it up and made the picture. It turned out to be the big picture of the year. We didn't get any help from anybody. And that's why I think I liked it best.

It was made in 1930 but not released until 1932. What held it up so long?
Censors. Hughes was fighting them. He'd fight anybody. Hughes wouldn't do what they wanted to do. I think the censors, in their stupid way, said that anybody who commits things like Scarface did had to pay for it. You had to show them. We fought them for about a year and finally ended up by making what they wanted us to make. I made a scene where he ended up in the gutter, in a pile of horse manure, and I said, 'Isn't that enough?' They said, 'No.' So they told me to make another ending. Paul Muni wasn't there, so I had to make an ending without the star. I used feet, a hangman's noose, everything to say that he was hung.

That isn't in the version that we see today. Now we see him dying on a street under a Cook's Tours sign that says 'The World Is Yours.' Wasn't there also a long, moralistic printed prologue?
Probably. There were a lot of things that I never saw. They made a lot of strange scenes. I didn't have anything to do with the scenes with the mayor of the city.

Those scenes are cut into the middle of the film, and they're very jarring. The mayor and a bunch of people are talking about how terrible Scarface is.
The censors put it in. I wouldn't have a damn thing to do with it. When we release the picture again, that stuff will be out.

Is it going to be redistributed?
We're working on it. The people who are running Howard's estate

16 *Scarface*: Paul Muni with George Raft.

17 *Scarface*: Paul Muni with Ann Dvorak.

are trying to make a better deal with me, so it depends who can hang out the longest. Hughes left word to confiscate all copies of the film, now that he's dead. They're trying to get ahold of *Scarface*.

Do the Hughes people have the original negative?
No, *I* have. That confuses them. I think they'll probably get it to be released. I'm not sure. [Hughes's Summa corporation eventually sold all rights to *Scarface* and other Hughes films to Universal, which made *Scarface* available again in 1979. Prior to that, it could be seen in this country only in bootleg versions.]

How did you get the idea for the film, from the Al Capone stories in the papers?
I wanted Ben Hecht to write on it, and he said, 'Sure, what are you going to make?' I said, 'A gangster picture.' He said, 'Hell, you don't want to make one of those things.' I said, 'Well, Ben, I've got an idea that the Borgia family is living in Chicago today. See, our Borgia is Al Capone, and his sister does the same incest thing as Lucretia Borgia.' And he said, 'Well, let's start tomorrow morning.' We did the script in eleven days. There was a young reporter, John Lee Mahin, who worked on it, and he had some good ideas [Mahin said in a 1980 interview that the analogy with the Borgias was suggested by Hecht, not by Hawks]. We knew just what we wanted. The original story [a novel by Armitage Trail] had two brothers in it. The script didn't have the brother.

What kind of research did you do?
I made a contact with one of the best newspapermen in Chicago so that we could use the newspaper wire. I could ask him about people and things. If a man came into my office and said, 'My name is James White, I was connected to the gang in Chicago. I wonder if I could talk to you,' I'd say, 'I'm sorry, Mr White, I'm so busy. Will you come tomorrow?' And by that time I would have gotten in touch with Chicago and said, 'Who the hell is James White?' So when he came in I'd say, 'Hello, Puggy.' 'How did you know my name?' I'd say, 'I know all about you.' He'd say, 'How do you know?' And I'd say, 'Oh . . . I know. I know that you started as a

bouncer and became a pimp, you ran a saloon, you carried a gun for so-and-so, did such-and-such a murder.' I'd get through and he'd say, 'I wasn't no pimp.' And I'd say, 'OK, what do you want? Want work to pay for your passage out here?' He'd say, 'Sure.' I'd say, 'How did you do such-and-such a thing?' And he told me quite a lot. Five or six of them came around and told me their stories. Of course, we took liberties; we did what we wanted to do.

Did you do the same kind of thing when you were preparing The Criminal Code *[1931]?*
Oh, yeah, we wrote a whole bunch of stuff for that because the last act was absolutely no good. But I liked the beginning, I liked the story. So I got twenty convicts, got 'em a room, gave 'em a lunch, gave 'em a drink. I sat down and said, 'I'm going to tell you guys a story, and I want you to decide how it ends. I'll go off until you decide.' I went off, and they talked for about an hour, and I came in and said, 'Are you ready to talk?' and they told me the whole ending, the whole last act. Then I had convicts working for me. One time they got bored with what they were doing, so I put 'em on a dog trot, and I said, 'You're going to keep trotting until you decide to behave, and anybody who stops is automatically fired.' So they made a couple of rounds of this place until they yelled out, 'Hey, mister, we'll be good!' I said, 'OK, let's hear it from everybody whether they'll be good.' And they would go by me saying, 'We'll be good, we'll be good.' So I stopped them, and we became pretty good friends.

One of the unusual things about Scarface *is that you look on the gangsters almost as little kids. They're treated not so much as vile murderers but as very childlike figures who couldn't quite comprehend the meaning of good.*
A great many of the gangsters that I met *were* pretty childish. I get awfully sick and tired of a lot of the gangster stuff that I see where everybody is growling at somebody and being the toughest guy in the world. These fellows were not that way. They were just like kids. We had fun doing it. When we conceived the idea that these fellows were childish, it helped us do some scenes. For instance, Ben Hecht

wrote Muni a scene when I told him I thought we ought to make a good scene out of when Capone discovered a machine gun. Ben said, 'What do you mean?' I said, 'Well, can't you write a scene like a kid finding a new toy?' 'Oh, yeah.' And he wrote a marvellous line – Muni came in with a machine gun and Johnny Lovo said, 'You murdering ape, you're going to take orders.' Muni said, 'This is the only thing that gives orders, Johnny. Get out of my way, I'm gonna spit.' The fellow jumped to one side, and the machine gun went off.

How did you find Muni?
After we did the script, we couldn't borrow any money, and we couldn't get an actor. I told Howard I was going to New York to see what I could do. I saw Muni in a Jewish theatre on 39th Street playing an old, old man. I asked him if he'd like to do the picture, and he said, 'I'm not that kind of a guy.' I said, 'Well, are you afraid to make a test?' 'No,' he said. So we built some clothes and made him look husky and put him on a four-inch platform. We got little people to play with him, and he made the test, and he was very pleased. Muni could do any damn thing that you could tell him to do. When he took the job, Muni told me, 'I'm not an athlete. I'm a completely sedentary man.' And I said, 'We'll take care of that.' He had to hit somebody. I don't know whether you remember, he hit somebody, and they went right over a table. I got a friend of mine who just happened to have been middleweight champion of the world, and I said, 'Can you teach this guy how to throw a punch?' He said sure. So for a couple of weeks, he'd put up his hand like this, and Muni would hit him. When we made the scene, the fellow started with his hand up and then took his hand away and took the punch. Muni just stood there staring at him. I said, 'Act, you son of a bitch! Act!'

Where did you get the rest of the cast?
I saw George Raft at a prize fight. At that time he was carrying a gun for the gangs. He said he'd like to act, so we got George. Ann Dvorak was a chorus girl at Metro-Goldwyn. I knew the vice-president of Metro, and I asked him if I couldn't borrow her. He said sure. I said, 'I don't mean just borrow her and then you get her back.

49

I want her after this is over.' He said OK. [Hawks used her again in *The Crowd Roars*.] Boris Karloff was utterly unknown, and he played just a little part. After that, I had an awful time with him. Every time I made a picture, he insisted on having a part in it. Vince Barnett had never acted. He and his father were professional – what would you call 'em? He would play a waiter at a party, and he'd spill things over you and crazy things like that, with his accent and his funny blank face. The only fellow in the picture who got any money was the fellow that played Johnny Lovo, the little fellow with black beady eyes. That was Osgood Perkins [Anthony Perkins's father]. He was a leading man on the New York stage. He wanted to come out and make a picture just for the fun of it. That picture was a lot of fun. Every member of the crew played a part in it. They really enjoyed the fact that they were independent.

How was Hughes to work with then?
He saw one of the first wrecks that we made, the result of the machine gun, and he said, 'My God, that was a good one! Why don't you make some more of 'em?' We made nineteen. Everybody in the crew would try to think of something that would happen. So, I'm rather fond of that picture.

Did you have any contact with Al Capone while making the picture?
While we were making it, five or six of them came out and said, 'The boss wants us to see the picture.' And I said, 'You go and tell him when it comes out, he can pay a dollar and buy a ticket. You don't scare me. Why the hell don't you come out and just *ask* to see it?' They reported to Capone that it was just great, and they invited me to Chicago to see him. They met me at the train, and they were late. One of the fellows said, 'There was a killing last night and we had to go to the funeral.' I said, 'Do I have to ride with you if there was a killing last night?' They said I could ride in a different car. But when we went into a café, they would sit with their backs to the wall, and I had my back to the door. We had some damn good-looking girls with us, a bit brassy but very pretty. When I saw Capone, we had tea, and he was dressed in a morning coat, striped trousers, a

carnation, being a very nice man, saying how much he liked the picture. I was with him two, three hours. Then he asked me to come again, and I stopped by there. But there was a shooting in Chicago, so they said that he couldn't come because he was hiding out in Atlantic City or something. Then he came to see me when I was working in Hollywood, and the cops came and arrested him right on the set.

So he did see Scarface?
Five or six times. He had his own print of it. He thought it was great. He'd say, 'Jesus Christ, you guys got a lot of stuff in that picture! How'd you know about that?' I said, 'Look – you know how somebody can't testify if he's a lawyer? Well, I'm a lawyer.' And he laughed. He didn't give a damn. Another famous gangster brought two very lovely daughters out to watch the movie and introduced himself to me. He said, 'Where'd you get that stuff in that killing?' I asked him, 'Why? Are you mad?' He said, 'No, I'm just curious.' I told him, and he laughed, and he said, 'That's the way we did the shooting. Why hasn't the picture played in Chicago?' I said, 'They won't let me.' He said, 'Do you *want* it to play?' I said yeah. And he said, 'Can I use your phone a minute?' When he finished he said, 'You can play it any time you want.'

You started directing The Outlaw *for Hughes in 1940 and then left after ten days. He completed it. What happened?*
I had a chance to do *Sergeant York* with Cooper, so I said to Hughes, 'You've always wanted to direct, why don't you finish this thing?' He said, 'Do you think I can?' I said, 'I'll tell you after you get through with it.' After he got through with it, I said, 'I don't know.' I didn't think it was too good.

Then you had a legal hassle with Hughes over his claim that you plagiarized The Outlaw *in making* Red River.
I had a hangover one Sunday morning [in 1930], and Hughes showed up at the house and said, 'I'm making a picture called *Hell's Angels*. I'm making a scene of a flyer getting shot in the chest, and his plane explodes. You've got the same scene in your picture [*The*

Dawn Patrol]. I don't want you to do it.' I said, 'Howard, I make pictures for a living, you make them for fun. I got a hangover. I'm not interested in talking about it.' So he got his writer to go to my secretary and offer her two hundred dollars for the script. She told me about it, and I had a couple of detectives hiding in her closet. When the guy offered her the money, they said, 'You're under arrest.' Hughes called me and said, 'Hey, you've got that writer of mine in jail.' And I said, 'You son of a bitch, he'll stay there.' He said, 'What did you do that for?' I said, 'I don't like anybody corrupting a nice girl. If you had wanted the script why didn't you ask me for it?' He said, 'Would you have given it to me?' I said, 'Sure, I would have. You can't own a scene like that. A person that gets shot riding in an airplane almost always gets shot in the chest.' So he was doing everything he could to keep our picture from coming out before his. People do strange things. As for the end of *Red River*, I told Hughes I didn't think he made the scene very good in *The Outlaw*, and I said, 'Some day I'll show you how to do it.' And I made it again. That made him mad. So he sued me to make me take out a line that said, 'Draw your gun.' Hughes sent down a battery of lawyers; we'd have won if we'd wanted to defend it, but finally I cut it out, and it played better without the line. I got some of the funniest telegrams from other directors – Billy Wilder sent me a telegram saying, 'I own the rights to say, "They went that-a-way."' And Frank Capra said, 'I own the rights to say "I love you."' It's quite a good collection. Hughes and I ended up friendly afterward.

How did you get along with him personally?
We played golf and lied to each other about our handicaps. He flew my airplane and I flew his. I went with him when he tested that speed plane that was better than anything that the Army or Navy had made. He called me up, and I flew down in my plane. He said, 'When I take off, I'd like to have you watch me.' So I said, 'OK, I'll get back there and start and get way up to speed. Then you judge when I'll be over you, because you're a lot faster than I am, and if you have to land, land in that bean field out there.' He said, 'Why do you say that?' I said, 'Well, I've landed in two or three of them, and they're a great place to land.' So he took off, and everything seemed

to be going all right, and then the cockpit cover flew off his airplane. He let the wheels up and landed in this bean field, slid right in, got out and waved to me. Then I went back and got a car to pick him up. He could fly, and he had a lot of guts. He was the only man who could ever have flown that airplane. Nothing on it was labelled. Nobody else could have known what the deuce to do.

When was the last time you saw him?
Hughes bought these hotels up in Vegas, and he heard I was up there. He asked me to come over and say hello to him. He said, 'What are you up here for?' I said, 'My youngster's driving in the Western Championship.' And he said, 'I'll see how he does.' Well, he won, so there was a note from Howard saying, 'Take him and a couple of the other boys to dinner and it's on me.' So I told the boys, 'As long as he's paying for the dinner, I'll back you fellows at roulette.' We took the numbers of each of their cars, and I bet on them, and they won, so each of the boys did pretty well. That was the last time I saw Hughes. I heard from him at other times. I had some letters from him. All I know is that he didn't want to be seen. He was losing weight – a skeleton – and he was very, very conscious of that.

9

Two Films with James Cagney

How did you get involved in two films at Warners with James Cagney, The Crowd Roars *and* Ceiling Zero?
When was *The Crowd Roars* made?
In 1932.
Well, I used to race for several years, but about that time I began to get interested again in cars. And no one had done a real story of racing, beginning on the little dirt tracks and moving on up to the Ascot night races and then on up to Indianapolis. It was pretty easy, because we had six or seven Indianapolis winners driving in the picture. They were very glad to do it. And we had a lot of fun making the dirt track things. We went up to Ventura, to a little horse track. We had a whole bunch of jalopies, and we started to race. I knew there was going to be trouble because so much dust came up; the second time around, they disappeared in the dust. You heard fenders crashing and fence posts going, and everything was a mess. We were blowing bugles, doing everything we could to stop the race. The dust cleared and nobody got hurt. There were some cars banged up. So we had to send up to town and get some stuff to lay the dust, and then went ahead and made the scenes. For the night racing at Ascot, we let gasoline loose on the track and had a fire going. That was pretty good racing stuff. Actually, the story of *The Crowd Roars* was almost the story of *The Barker*, a play Walter Huston did where he played a circus barker. He was living with a girl, and his son was coming. It was practically the same plot that we used there. We laid it in a racing background. We had a lot of help – the Dusenberg brothers, who made the Dusenberg cars, got interested and came over. Augie Dusenberg made a tow bar so that we could tow a car up to 120 miles an hour and release it automatically at any place we wanted to and have a wheel come off that car. We knew

right where the accidents were gonna take place. So we didn't have any accidents in making the picture. We had some narrow escapes. And we had some strange people who were driving. We had one man, Joe Russo, who could drive blindfolded; I rode around the track at 120 miles an hour with him, and he was blindfolded. He would say, 'We're going to pass a tin can sitting on a fence post – now!' And it would be right opposite. He steered by the feel of the track. And Cagney was so much fun to work with because you never knew what Cagney was gonna do. When I work with Cary Grant, I can go home and write a scene for Cary and know how he's gonna handle it the next day, but Cagney had these funny little attitudes, you know, the way he held his hands and things like that. I tried to make the most of them, and I think we did pretty well even though I didn't know how he worked.

Was it you who cast Cagney?
Yeah. The moment I saw Cagney I wanted him for a picture, because he did things completely differently from anybody else. And I love that kind of stuff.

Was it The Public Enemy [1931] *you had seen him in?*
I couldn't tell you what I saw, but I saw him in a picture just before I cast him. Bogart and Cagney were two actors that Warner Brothers just fell heir to. They just came in and found themselves. Cagney got the part in *The Public Enemy* because he was so much better than the fellow [Eddie Woods] who was playing it that they switched him right in the middle of making the picture, gave him the good part. You see, Bogart and Cagney are great personalities *and* good actors.

I've talked to other directors who worked with Cagney – Raoul Walsh, Bill Wellman – and I asked them how it was to work with him, and they said, 'Well, Cagney was great.' They can't explain it beyond that. What made *him great?*
Jim Cagney worked with movement. He didn't work with lines. I don't remember him ever suggesting a line – it's the way he *does* the line, the stuff you feed him, that makes him so good. Whenever I work with a fellow who was as good as Cagney – let's include

18 *The Crowd Roars*: James Cagney with Eric Linden and Joan Blondell.

19 *The Crowd Roars*: On the track.

Bogart there – I make sure that they feel free to try anything. Because I can always tell them, 'I don't like that.' We try things one way, we try things another way. Every scene almost, we'd say, 'How was that?' 'Pretty good. It's a little *usual*. Can't you think of some different way of doing it?' And we'd sit there, and I don't know who'd think of it, he would think of it or I would think of it, and we'd do it. And the reactions and things would change the scene a little bit. Not really change it, but it would make an interesting scene.

In The Crowd Roars, *Cagney cries on the lap of Ann Dvorak. Was that in the original script?*
Oh, I don't think so. I've seen plenty of men cry. When I get somebody who was good enough – I tried it with Dick Barthelmess in *Dawn Patrol*, and he sounded like a cow mooing. So I said, 'This isn't gonna work very well, you're not a good cryer.' But Cagney was great, and Grant was great doing it in *Only Angels Have Wings*.

How did you get involved with Ceiling Zero?
I saw the play in New York, and I thought it would make a good picture. We changed it quite a little bit. *Ceiling Zero* was written by Spig Wead, a famous flyer, a former aviation racer, who broke his back falling down the cellar stairs one night and was confined to a wheelchair [his story was told by John Ford in *The Wings of Eagles*, 1957, with John Wayne]. He wrote a damn good play, but he always wanted his men to be very bravado. It was never under-played. I changed that. We kind of took off on his writing from the things he would have liked to have done. He loved women, and I think that finished women for him, so his heroes were always womanizers. The play *Ceiling Zero* was written for a man who made passes continually. Well, Cagney made one pass at the girl, and I said to him, 'Jim, we're in trouble. You're too smart to make a second pass. There's about three of them written in the script, and it's getting ridiculous. You make your first pass so good, what are you gonna do?' He said, 'I guess I didn't read it carefully.' I said, 'Well, let's stop and think what we're gonna do.' We all sat around,

and finally a little property man said, 'If I miss out on my first pass, I say to the girl, "Look, I was wrong." I apologize, and then I blame everything on her. I say, "I promise to behave myself too." It always worked.' So I said, 'We're off,' and we just worked on that basis. In the scenario, Cagney gave the girl the key to his room. In the picture, the girl gave Cagney the key to her room. It was all switched around. We had fun doing it.

10

William Faulkner

Bill and I were very good friends. We hunted and fished a lot. He worked with me on, oh, half a dozen pictures. If I wanted a scene or a story, I'd call up Bill and get it. He could write almost anything. Bill, like a lot of authors, didn't make any money until paperbacks came in, and until France and other countries found him. He was too hard to read. So he needed money, and very often he'd let me know, and I'd see that he'd do a scene. Like the death scene of the pilot in *Air Force*; he wrote it overnight. He worked on *The Big Sleep* with Leigh Brackett; they did the script in eight days. It's a great script. Actually, I had a good deal to do with people discovering Faulkner. I read a book called *Soldiers' Pay*, one of his first books, and then I read another one, and I bought 'Turn About', a short story of his. And I was back in New York working with Hecht and MacArthur, and they hung around with the so-called intelligentsia, the literary crowd, and one day I said, 'Have you fellows ever read anything by William Faulkner?' Nobody'd ever heard of Faulkner. I said, 'I just read a book you should read, called *Soldiers' Pay*.' They borrowed the book and discovered Faulkner.

What writers do you admire besides Faulkner?
I like the fellow who wrote *The Big Sleep* [Raymond Chandler]. I like Hemingway. I like Dashiell Hammett.

What contribution do you think Faulkner made to your films?
We seemed to talk the same language. He knew what I wanted. Bill drank too much, but when he wasn't drinking he was awful good. He wrote *Pylon*, which wasn't an awful good book because he got drunk when he went down to an air show to see what it was like. He had kind of a hazy idea of it. I told him to write it. I got mad at him one

20 *Land of the Pharaohs*: Jack Hawkins on the throne.

day and told him I got so sick and tired of the goddam inbred people he was writing about. I said, 'Why don't you write about some decent people, for goodness' sake?' 'Like who?' I said, 'Well, you fly around, don't you know some pilots or something that you can write about?' And he thought a while, and he said, 'Oh, I know a good story. Three people – a girl and a man were wingwalkers, and the other man was a pilot. The girl was gonna have a baby, and she didn't know which one was the father.' I said, 'That sounds good,' and he wrote *Pylon* from that. Faulkner was very smart, he told it through the eyes of the drunken reporter. I didn't think it was much good, though.

Douglas Sirk made a fine movie out of it, The Tarnished Angels [*1958*].
I didn't see that.

Faulkner worked on the screenplay of Today We Live [1933], *the film you made at MGM from 'Turn About'.*

I thought it'd be nice to get him out and let him write on it. He did a beautiful job. We got all ready to make the picture, and they called me in and said, 'You're about ready to start, aren't you?' I said yeah. 'Who have you got?' I said, 'I've got Gary Cooper and two young fellas, Bob Young and Franchot Tone.' They said, 'Well, you've got Joan Crawford too.' I said, 'No, there's no girl in the picture.' They said, 'There is one now. We'll lose a million dollars if we don't have something for Joan Crawford. So you're stuck.' I called Faulkner in and told him, 'Bill, we gotta put a girl in this story.' And he said, 'Holy smoke!' We put the girl in, and the picture was quite successful.

To Have and Have Not has been described as the only film that had two Nobel Prize-winning writers working on the script – Hemingway and Faulkner.

Bill loved working on it because it was Hemingway's. He wanted to change it. I'd say, 'Can't you find something of Hemingway's to change?' We had a lot of fun. Did I ever tell you the story about Gable and Faulkner? Faulkner and I were going dove hunting down in Imperial Valley. Gable called up and said, 'What are you doing?' I told him. He said, 'Can I go?' I said, 'Sure, if you can get over here in a hurry.' So we hired a station wagon, and we started down with a couple of bottles of bourbon. We were coming through Palm Springs, and the talk was about writing. Gable asked Faulkner who the good writers were. And Faulkner said, 'Thomas Mann, Willa Cather, John Dos Passos, Ernest Hemingway, and myself.' Gable looked at him and said, 'Oh, do you write, Mr Faulkner?' And Faulkner said, 'Yeah. What do *you* do, Mr Gable?' I don't think Gable ever read a book, and I don't think Faulkner ever went to see a movie. So they might have been on the level.

You also had Faulkner as a scriptwriter on Land of the Pharaohs.

We were going to work on it, and he was flying over. They took him to Switzerland because of the weather. So he had a few drinks too many, and he went up to Montmartre, because he knew Montmartre. He somehow fell down and got a little bloody. I woke up, and two great big gendarmes were bringing him into my hotel room. They were giving him a lot of attention because he had a *Légion d'Honneur* button in his lapel. They dropped him and got the chair kind of bloody. I had to get somebody to take care of him for a week or two, and then he came out of it and started to work. We had a lot of fun, and we had a pretty good premise of a story. We started to work on it with Harry Kurnitz, a very fine playwright, and Faulkner said, 'I don't know how a pharoah talks.' I said, 'Well, I don't know, I never talked to one.' And he said, 'Is it all right if I write him like a Kentucky colonel?' And Kurnitz said, 'I can't do it like a Kentucky colonel, but I'm a student of Shakespeare. I think I could do it as though it were *King Lear*.' So I said, 'Well, you fellows go ahead, and I'll rewrite your stuff.'

They did it, and I messed it up, and . . . we didn't know what a pharaoh *did*.

I thought the picture was great as far as masses of people and things like that, but I made a mistake: I should have had somebody in there that you were rooting for. Everybody was a son of a bitch.

Was your unhappy experience on Land of the Pharaohs *the reason you waited four years before you made your next picture,* Rio Bravo?
I did such a bad job that I thought I'd better sit back and take a good look at the way things were going. It sort of gave me a fresh attitude.

11

MGM and *Viva Villa!*

Metro was the best studio in the world for getting a script and handing it to a director with it all cast and the sets all built – they had the best set designers, and they had good writers – but I don't think that an independent worked very well over there. I didn't make much at Metro. I made the one with Joan Crawford, I told you, the Faulkner story which was messed up. And I made *Viva Villa!*, which was messed up [Hawks was fired during the shooting and replaced by Jack Conway], so I was glad to get out of that goddam place.

You also directed part of The Prizefighter and the Lady *without credit for MGM in 1933. Why was that?*
The Prizefighter and the Lady was a story that I worked on. It was written for Gable and Harlow. Gable was the dominant one, and Harlow was the empty-headed blonde. They cast it with Max Baer and Myrna Loy – *complete* opposites. In other words, Max Baer was the stooge, and Loy was the lady, the prizefighter and the lady. I said, 'I don't want to make the picture.' I wouldn't make it with them. And they said, 'Will you help out, do a couple of weeks' work, give Baer a start, teach him a little about acting? Then Woody Van Dyke will take over.' I said sure. [John Lee Mahin, who wrote the script, disputed this version, contending that Hawks was fired after two days of shooting because he worked too slowly. Hawks was fired from *Viva Villa!* after completing location work in Mexico; Mahin said Hawks and studio chief Louis B. Mayer came to blows over Hawks's shooting pace. Hawks claimed the fight was over Mayer's demand that he fire actor Lee Tracy. See p. 71.]

What was it like working with Thalberg?
Jack Warner was a showman, Harry Cohn was a showman. They

21 *Viva Villa!*: Wallace Beery as Pancho Villa.

22 *Viva Villa!*: A Hawks film taken over by Jack Conway.

let you alone. But Thalberg would let you make a picture and then would get you in very nicely and say, 'Look, we've got the sets, we've got the people, everybody's under contract. Now, I think you could do a little bit better with this.' And he'd make about ten days' work over again and make a whole different picture out of it. He didn't do that with any of mine. We were good friends. We used to talk things over before we made it.

Tell me about your experiences on Viva Villa!

When we went down to Mexico to make *Viva Villa!*, they had some sort of gangsters down there, and I was taken out by these gangsters to meet the man who shot Villa. We were going on horses, it was the only way we could get up there. They all carried guns, so I carried a gun. I used to be a damn good shot with a revolver. I took the gun out and shot at a tin can and made it roll along the ground. Shot again and made it keep on going, put the gun back. That was all luck, you know. Oh, golly, they looked at me – they weren't going to start anything if I could shoot *that* way. One guy down there was going to show me how to kill somebody. I'd made *Scarface* and, you know, they thought – he got hold of a poor little taxi driver and was gonna shoot him. I stopped him. Then all his bodyguards pointed guns at me. I said, 'Wait a minute, wait a minute. When I met him he had a pink leather suit on. I'd much rather he'd be wearing a leather suit when he killed a man than this awful blue suit.' 'Oh, OK, OK,' he said, and he came running back and said that the pink suit had gone to the laundry, but when it came back again he would kill a man while wearing it. No kidding. Oh, hell! We had the soldiers and the peons, we would search them all two or three times, and they'd whittle wooden bullets, which, if you put a gun close enough to somebody, would go into his stomach. And they would stick bullets up their rectums and pull 'em out and shoot somebody. There were people shot every day when we were making the movie. It was crazy in those days. We were making scenes in a little town about two hundred miles out of Mexico City, and that was a long way out then. We couldn't get any food. We had two-day-old box lunches sent out from Mexico City. Couldn't eat any food out there. Lived on oranges and brandy. But we were making some scenes and

66

working on a railroad cut – you know, where the railroad runs through and the sides are steep – and a fellow came out and shoved a gun at me and started to yell something. I just turned and hit him, and he went over and lit on his head on the railroad track. I never heard whether he died, or what happened. I said, 'What the hell was he yelling?' They told me that he said, 'This is for the revolution!' We were making another scene one time and some shooting took place about half of a short block away. People went running out firing guns. This was for real. A car passed us one day going too fast – it rolled over and through a fence. We got over there, and a guy crawled out of it, looked back in, pulled out a gun, and blew his brains out. It was nutty. Finally after ten weeks Eddie Mannix [general manager of MGM Studios] came and said, 'This isn't working out, Howard, you can go.' I said, 'Eddie, I've suffered for ten weeks here, so I want to be paid for ten more weeks.' He said, 'OK.'

12

Twentieth Century

23 *Twentieth Century*: Hawks with Carole Lombard and John
Barrymore.

I went from Metro over to Harry Cohn [president of Columbia], who told me any time that I wanted to make a picture, just come in and tell him what it was, and I could start on it. I told him I wanted to do *Twentieth Century*.

It was based on a play by Hecht and MacArthur.
They wrote it for Gregory Ratoff's wife, Eugenie Leontovich, who was a stylized Russian actress. I called them and asked them to do the script – there was good money in it for them – for Sadie Glutz instead of a Russian. They said that would be fine. They thought that would be much better. The next day I got on the train and went back to Hecht and MacArthur; we wrote the script in five days. We had a lot of help – we'd promised to help Billy Rose, and he was the world's champion shorthand writer, so we just talked dialogue, and Billy wrote it down, and a girl sat up all night and copied it. It was a very funny script. I got Barrymore and Carole Lombard, and we made the picture in three weeks' time. Ten weeks to a day from the day I left Metro, I was going to the preview that night. I called Eddie Mannix up, and I said, 'Do you want to go to a preview tonight?' 'What is it?' I said, 'It's a pretty good picture, you'd better come and see it.' When he saw the title, he said, 'Did you make this from the time you left our place?' and I said, 'Yeah.'

Twentieth Century *deals with stage actors and producers. Are any of the characters based on people you know?*
Nobody. I'd never been backstage in my life. When we came to the backstage scenes, I told Barrymore, 'Now, look, you know eight times as much about this as I do. You stage it.' 'OK,' he said, and he staged it, did the chalk marks and all that. The rest of the picture was easy, because those two people were just remarkable. When I first met Barrymore, he said, 'I'll come down to your office and talk to you about the story,' and I said, 'I'd like to see your house. I've heard about it.' So I went up there and told him the story, and he said, 'Mr Hawks, just why do you think I would be any good in this picture?' I said, 'It's the story of the greatest ham in the world, and God knows you fit that.' And he said, 'I'll do the picture.' He never even read it. And it was the girl's first picture. She was a second

69

24 *Twentieth Century*: Ralph Forbes, Lombard and Barrymore.

25 *Twentieth Century*: The chalk marks scene.

cousin of mine and an amazing personality who'd never acted and couldn't act anyway. I remember when we started working, I told her if she acted I'd fire her. And she said, 'OK, I'll do anything that comes into my mind.' I said, 'That's what I want you to do.' She would just throw lines at him so fast that he didn't know what to do sometimes. It was so fast, *I* didn't understand it part of the time.

Did you have any problems with Barrymore's drinking when you were making the film?
I did lose one day when he got tight. He said, 'I'll give you two days free to make up for it.' But he worked so hard he was entitled to a day off. I've found out that people like that – I've heard that Bob Mitchum drank – if they're busy, if they've got something good to do, they won't do it. Lee Tracy was a drunk. I had him in *Viva Villa!*, and he never once had any trouble with it. [However, after shooting was finished, Tracy was fired for urinating on the Mexican Army from his hotel balcony. Stuart Erwin replaced him in the part.]

It took a while for Twentieth Century *to catch on at the box office, didn't it?*
It started very slowly, and then it started to grow. The public wasn't ready for seeing two stars act like comedians the way those two did. I don't think John Barrymore ever made a complete idiot out of himself until he did *Twentieth Century*. They didn't have leading men and leading women make damn fools of themselves like they did in that picture. The same thing happened when we did *Bringing Up Baby*. Cary Grant certainly never did slapstick comedy until we did *Bringing Up Baby*. It's just a question of realizing that everybody is falling into a pattern, and you get sick and tired of that pattern, and you do anything you can to get out of that. What do you call pictures that become –

Cult classics?
No – classics.

13

Comedy and Tragedy

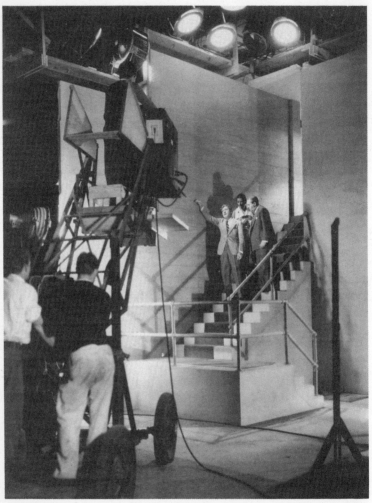

26 *Twentieth Century*: Shooting John Barrymore and Walter Connolly.

Your attitude is basically comic, even in a tragic situation. For instance, Al Capone is not really a funny story, but you made a comedy out of it.

Well, would you rather see something dead serious or laugh at something? In the first place, true drama is awfully close to being comedy. The greatest drama in the world is really funny. A man who loses his pants out in front of a thousand people – he's suffering the tortures of the damned, but he's awfully funny doing it. I had a damned good teacher, Chaplin. Probably our greatest comic. And everything he did was tragedy. He made things funny out of tragedy. I work a lot on that. I wanted to do *Don Quixote* with Cary Grant and Cantinflas, and people said, 'But that isn't a comedy – that's a tragedy.' I'd have to go into a long explanation. I think we could have a lot of fun with it. I think that Don Quixote's the basis for the Chaplin character. Maybe we'll do it; I don't know. Before Cary gets too old or I get too old, we hope to do it.

Your movies have been compared to Buster Keaton's in some ways, for the visual sparsity, the lack of frills. Do you like Keaton's movies?

I like Keaton's. But Chaplin is the best of 'em all.

I would have thought you'd prefer Keaton, because Chaplin is very sentimental, and Keaton is sort of tough, like your characters.

Well, I couldn't do the sentimental type, and so I happen to like 'em better.

You're famous for taking a scene that has elements of pain and humiliation, such as the finger amputation in The Big Sky *or the 'Who's Joe?' scene in* Only Angels Have Wings, *and either playing it lightly or for outright slapstick. Can you explain why you like to do something like that?*

You're looking for something new to be funny. The only time John Wayne ever objected to a scene was on our first picture, *Red River.* I said, 'Duke, I've got a good idea. You get your finger caught between the rope and the saddle horn, and it's all smashed. You show it to Walter Brennan, and he says, "That finger ain't gonna be much good to you." And you say, "No, I guess it isn't." So Brennan calls for somebody and says, "Stick an iron in the fire. Get a block of wood, and get a nice big jug of whiskey." And then you get drunk, and they heat up the iron to cauterize the thing. Brennan starts sharpening his knife. Then we'll fuss around in there until somebody says, "I think he's about ready for it." And then they'll hold your finger over a chopping block, and cut it off. They say, "He never even felt it." And just when everything is very happy, why, you say, "Where's my finger? A man ought have his finger. He should be buried with it, whole." And you all end up on your behinds looking in the ashes.' He said. 'You think that's *funny*?' 'Oh,' I said, 'if you're not good enough then we won't do it. I'll do it sometime with somebody who's a better actor.' So I did it with Kirk Douglas, who is not as good an actor, but Kirk did it, and it was very funny. Duke saw it, and he told me, 'If you tell me a funeral is funny, I'll do a funeral.' One of the best scenes that I ever made was in *Rio Bravo*. Wayne hit a fellow across the face the most horrible way. Dean Martin said, 'Hey, take it easy.' And Wayne said, 'I'm not gonna hurt him.' The audience thought it was funny. In *Rio Lobo*, we set a man on fire. He tries to hit Wayne with an oil lamp, and Wayne knocks him against a wall, and the lamp breaks, and the oil spills over him. He's burning, and somebody goes to pick up a blanket to put the thing out. Wayne says, 'Let him burn.' And the other fellow [Jack Elam] says, 'Don't let him burn so much he can't sign the papers we want him to sign.' And, I don't know, to me that was funny.

Why do you think it is?
I've seen so many people laugh at violence when it happens. Kind of hysterical laughter. It's the easiest time for you to get a laugh. I'm getting goddam sick of these pictures, you know, nothing but violence. Peckinpah and I believe in exactly the opposite thing. I like it when it's so quick that you say, 'My God, did it really happen?' And it's much easier to get comedy if you don't start out trying to be funny. That's a particular theory of mine, that if people start a picture and they have a funny main title, a lot of funny things, it's as much as to say, 'We expect you to laugh.' I think that's committing suicide. They're going to go against it. So I start out and try and get

their attention with a good dramatic sequence, and then find a place to start getting some laughs. We did that with *Rio Bravo*, we did that with *El Dorado*, and we did it very much with *Rio Lobo*. It starts off being *very* serious, and then before the audience realizes it, you're starting in having some fun. Look at *His Girl Friday*. It's the story of a poor little guy, an escaped murderer, and his girl commits suicide. Now, you can't tell anybody that you're gonna make a comedy about an escaped murderer. It has no relation to a comedy except for the way that Hecht and MacArthur treated the thing.

It's funny because it's done from the viewpoint of the reporters, who are not involved in the main action, at least initially. But if you were doing the story from the viewpoint of the escaped murderer, wouldn't it tend to be a tragedy then?
Oh, yes, it certainly would. It's all in the point of view.

Some of your comedies actually get pretty grim at times. Such as Bringing Up Baby *or* I Was a Male War Bride. *The predicaments the people get into become rather harrowing.* Bringing Up Baby, *particularly in the later scenes, is so dark photographically, it's lit almost like a tragedy.*
Well, it was pretty sad for Cary Grant going around on his hands and knees looking for a bone.

How do you write comic dialogue?
I don't use funny lines. They're not funny unless you see them. Some friends once came up to me and said they saw two of the greatest comics you've ever seen in your life – Rowan and Martin. So I went to see them expecting somebody funny. I didn't see anyone funny at all. All they had was a few funny lines. They'd been rehearsing those lines for two years. You can split an audience right down the middle, and half of them will laugh at one line and half at another; that isn't good enough. I can't remember ever using a funny line in a picture. They *become* funny because of their attitudes, because of the attitudes that work against what they're trying to say. And to me, that's the funniest comedy in the world. In *Rio Bravo*, the fellow in jail said about Walter Brennan, 'Look, that guy, he – don't trust him!

He'll shoot me! He's crazy!' Brennan laughed. He thought that was marvellous, to be called crazy. He said, 'You know, I'm just nuts!' People laughed at that. Because usually the idea is for a man when he's called crazy to get angry; Brennan was delighted. Those are the things that I think are funny. James Caan was funny as the Chinaman in *El Dorado*. What did he do that was funny? What was the funny line? It was just the silliness, the ridiculous quality of doing that. You know, and starting off on a rescue blowing a bugle and carrying a bow and arrow, all of that is such ridiculous, crazy stuff. I prefer making comedies, but the hardest thing in the world is to find a funny story. I found a lot of phony funny stories. Interesting thing – the last Oscar [1974], everybody said *The Exorcist* was gonna win. I made quite a little money. They offered me five to one and ten to one and even twenty to one: I said *The Sting*. And they came to me afterwards and said, 'Why did you say that?' And I said, 'There's only been two good comedies made in four years. One was *What's Up Doc?*, the other was *The Sting*. None of the rest have been worth calling comedies.' I think people are so damned anxious to see comedies, to laugh, I was sure it was gonna win. *What's Up Doc?* was a triumph for Bogdanovich. Because Barbra Streisand isn't funny. Ryan O'Neal is not funny. And yet the picture is funny. It was all sight gags, and they were damn good. I saw the picture in Spain, and when they laugh all the way through it and they don't understand one title, then you know it's a funny picture.

What did you think when people said What's Up Doc? *was stolen from* Bringing Up Baby?
I told Peter, 'You made a mistake in telling 'em where you stole it from. I didn't tell 'em where *I* stole it from.' And I told Peter the only mistake he made in doing the picture was that he didn't steal the dinosaur too. When Peter wanted to make *What's Up Doc?*, he showed me some tests of Ryan O'Neal and Barbra Streisand, and I said, 'Jesus Christ, this is gonna be horrible, Peter. They're trying to be funny. Take 'em in and show 'em *Bringing Up Baby*. Make 'em run it two or three times. Lecture 'em. Don't let 'em try to be funny.' Well, they got away with it, but it would have been awful if it had been the way the test scene was first made.

14

Grant and Hepburn

In your comedies, you always have the woman pursuing a very shy man. It's unusual on the screen to have men be so shy and women be so aggressive. Yet you were doing it in the late 1920s and 1930s before that kind of thing was seen much in comedies.

You take a professor, and you use the girl's part to knock his dignity down – Katie Hepburn and Cary were a great combination [in *Bringing Up Baby*]. It's pretty hard to think of anybody but Cary Grant in that type of stuff. He was so far the best that there isn't anybody to be compared to him. But I can almost make you eat those words. In *His Girl Friday*, that was a battle from beginning to end; Rosalind Russell didn't have an easy job at all. He was giving her a really tough time. Even in the end of the picture, where they were going off very happily, she was having trouble carrying the luggage. He said, 'Can't you do a better job of carrying that?' But I will admit that in most of the comedies, the woman had the dominant part. Because Cary is such a great receiver. He was so marvellous. We finally got so that I'd say, 'Cary, this is a good chance to do Number Seven.' Number Seven was trying to talk to a woman who was doing a lot of talking. We'd just do Number Seven. And he'd have to find variations on that. He and Hepburn were just great together. It was such a funny story, it was easy to be funny in it. I bought a short story written by a girl [Hagar Wilde]. I got the girl to come over, and she didn't know anything about pictures. But I wanted to keep exactly the same thought, that method of treating it. She had the characters for both Hepburn and Grant so well. So Dudley Nichols worked with her on the script. They worked right together. And he was awful good.

27 *Bringing Up Baby*: Cary Grant and Katharine Hepburn – 'You use the girl's part to knock his dignity down.'

28 *His Girl Friday*: Cary Grant and Rosalind Russell – 'In most of the comedies, the woman had the dominant part.'

29   *I Was a Male War Bride*: Cary Grant and Ann Sheridan – 'Just act like a man in woman's clothes.'

The scene you use in some of the comedies with Grant dressing up in women's clothing, such as when he wears the negligée in Bringing Up Baby, *was that done to humiliate the character to the utmost possible degree?*

The girl was playing a part of someone without a care in the world, and everything that she did got him farther and farther and farther into trouble. He stepped on her dress, he bitched up a golf game, she had a leopard – she just put him on a hook. It's logical that one of the craziest things was to put him in a woman's negligée. Anything we could do to humiliate him, to put him down and let her sail blithely along, made it what I thought was funny. I think it's fun to have a woman dominant and let the man be funniest. Katie and Rosalind Russell and Ann Sheridan in *I Was a Male War*

Bride did their share in being funny, but they played much straighter and left the other stuff to Cary. In *Male War Bride*, Cary was gonna put on a woman's uniform and be feminine. And he practised little tricks, worked on 'em and everything, and I said, 'Hey hey, hey, don't work on it. We're not gonna do that.' 'What do you mean?' 'Well,' I said, 'just act like a man in woman's clothes.' 'Oh, now, you're missing something there, Howard.' We'd gotten to Germany by that time, and the generals gave a party. I got on a WAC's outfit and a red wig, and I want to tell you, I looked funnier than Grant did. I came in, pulled out a cigar and said, 'Got a light, general?' He didn't know who or what I was. He thought I was a WAC. Cary was having convulsions, and he said, 'You sold me, I know just what to do.' You make the wig out of a horse's tail. You show a horse's behind and dissolve to Cary, and he's just sitting there. He doesn't have to do anything. Cary and I have a lot of fun. He gets mad in a scene. I said, 'Can't you think of a better way of getting mad than that?' I'd name two or three actors he doesn't like. 'That's the way to do it.' Then somebody would say, 'I know a man who when he would get mad he would whinny like a horse – *whoo, whoo, whoo* – just like that.' 'Well, that's fine, I'll do that,' he'd say.

How was Ann Sheridan to work with?
Great. I made a test of Ann Sheridan on a picture called *The Road to Glory* [1936, a different story from Hawks's silent film with the same title], playing the French girl. And she was fresh out of Texas, with a real Texas accent. I went over to talk to Jack Warner, and I said, 'Jack, I made a test of a girl today who can be *really* good. She's no good for what I want, but you should sign her.' He said, 'OK, send her over, and I'll sign her.' And she outlived some of the worst pictures you've ever known and became good. People liked her. They made her a star in spite of the bad pictures. Oh, she was quick and good and everything. And when we made *Male War Bride* she wasn't so young. She'd been through the mill by that time. But if you're going to make a good picture with Cary Grant, you'd better have somebody who's pretty damn good along with him. Christ, that picture took a year to make. Cary got yellow jaundice, Ann

30 *I Was a Male War Bride*: Hawks with Grant and Sheridan.

31 Hawks with Grant shooting *Monkey Business*.

Sheridan got pneumonia, I got some strange itch from sitting around. I got an itch that started on the top of my head and went right through my balls and everything down to my feet. All they knew about it was that soldiers in the Pacific got the same itch, and they cured it by going in the sea water. So I got big bags of salt and put it in the bathtub and lay in there and soaked. It cured me. Cary was out for six months. I had to wait; couldn't do anything. It was two-thirds done. Cary ran into a haystack on a motorcycle and came out weighing twenty pounds less.

How was Hepburn to work with on Bringing Up Baby?
We had trouble with Kate at first. The great trouble is people trying to be funny. If they don't try to be funny, then they are funny. I couldn't do any good with her, so I went over to an actor who was a comic for the Ziegfeld Follies and everything, Walter Catlett, and I said, 'Walter, have you been watching Miss Hepburn?' He said, 'Yeah.' 'Do you know what she's doing?' 'Yeah.' And I said, 'Will you tell her?' He said, 'No.' 'Well,' I said, 'supposing she asks you to tell her?' 'Well, then I'll have to tell her.' So I went over to Kate, and I said, 'We're not getting along too well on this thing. I'm not getting through to you, but there's a man here who I think could. Do you want me to talk to him?' She came back from talking with him and said, 'Howard, hire that guy and keep him around here for several weeks, because I need him.' And from that time on, she knew how to play comedy better, which is just to read lines. I can tell you another little story about Katie. Katie was making a lot of noise on the set one day, and we couldn't quiet her down. The assistant director called 'Quiet!' a couple of times, and finally I motioned him, 'Sit down here and watch.' So Katie all of a sudden turned around and said, 'What's the matter?' I said, 'You're acting a good part of a parrot, and if you're going to keep on doing it, we'll just sit here and watch you.' She said, 'I want to talk to you.' So we went behind the set and she said, 'Howard, you can't talk that way to me. I've got a lot of friends here.' I looked up on the scaffold at the electrician, and I said to him, 'If you had the choice of dropping a lamp on Miss Hepburn or me, who would you drop it on?' And he said, 'Get out of the way, Hepburn!' Katie was just marvellous. She said, 'I guess

I'm wrong.' From that time on we got along beautifully, no trouble at all. They're great people.

I spoke with Cary Grant recently, and I told him I wish he'd do another picture. But he said the only way he'd do a part would be if he could play it in a wheelchair, like Hitchcock did with his cameo in Topaz.
He's trying to be nice. He just doesn't want to make anything.

Yet women find him terribly attractive today.
I know it. I called Cary recently and asked him how he was doing with the girls. He said, 'Better than ever.'

What if you were to cast him as an older guy like himself and pair him with a young girl?
He doesn't want to make a picture with a young girl. I had a good script, *Man's Favorite Sport?*; he'd have been great in it. He just said, 'I'm not gonna play with three young girls.' I said, 'I'm not gonna get three old hags to play them.'

He would have been better than Rock Hudson.
Well, Rock tried hard, and he worked hard, he did everything he could, but Rock is not a comedian. And when you have visualized one person in it, and you're trying to get that, it's an awful job to do it because you just don't come out right. And even then we ended up with a pretty good picture.

15

Working with Writers: II

In *Only Angels Have Wings*, I knew every character personally that was in that picture. I knew how they talked. And if they began to talk too much because the writer [Jules Furthman] put in too much, I'd just say 'Cut it out,' then we'd get down to real lines. If you've seen the picture lately, you may remember Richard Barthelmess's part. I knew the fellow that jumped out of an airplane and left somebody behind to get killed. He spent the rest of his life trying to make up for that, and he got killed, finally, trying to make up for it. One critic said that usually you could count on my pictures not going too far, but in *Only Angels Have Wings* I went too far. I wrote him a letter and said there wasn't one single scene in the whole picture that wasn't real. I told him how I got the idea for the story at a party one night. I was with a Mexican bush pilot. We were flying around Mexico landing in washes and having a lot of fun. He told me a marvellous thing I couldn't put in the picture. He went to a dinner where there was a very attractive girl who had been married for a year to a fellow with a burnt face and great eyes. A fellow got up at the dinner and made a speech. He said, 'A year ago tonight we were celebrating the marriage. About one o'clock you shoved us all out. You went to bed about two minutes past. Then you got up at ten minutes past one, and then you had at it again a bit later.' He told the story of the whole wedding night, and the girl said, 'You son of a bitch, you were peeping!' He said no, and brought out a graph that was made from a German machine that you attach to your airplane. It shows when you started the motor, when you bounced while taking off, when you got up. And he'd hung it under the bed. The girl hung up the graph; she was so proud of it. That's where I got the story of *Only Angels Have Wings*.

32 *Red River*: The beginning.

The idea of a coward who has to redeem himself years later is quite reminiscent of Joseph Conrad's Lord Jim. *You produced a film of* Lord Jim *that Victor Fleming directed for Paramount in 1925, didn't you?*
Yes, bought it and produced it.

There was something that attracted you then to the story of Lord Jim, *and in 1939 you echoed it in your own way.*
Well, I steal from myself all the time.

How do you handle it when you're dealing with events that happened in the past that are haunting some of the characters? You have to provide the audience with explanations of what happened in the past, but it gets boring if you just tell it in words.
If the thing is worth photographing, you can figure a way to photograph it. I liked the beginning of *Red River*.

With John Wayne leaving the girl?
Leaving the girl and feeling that he was responsible for her death.
And I like the way we revealed her death.

With the bracelet.
Yeah, and then I like the way it came up later on, where the other
girl said, 'You felt like you had knives in you.' That recalled the past.
We never went *back* to the past. I don't remember a picture that I've
ever made that has gone back to the past.

What's wrong with flashbacks?
What's good about 'em? If you're not good enough to tell a story
without having flashbacks, why the hell do you try to tell them? Oh,
I think some extraordinarily good writer can figure out some way of
telling a story in flashbacks, but I hate them. Just like I hate screwed
up camera angles.

In Only Angels Have Wings, *you only hint at the shame in
Barthelmess's past. The characters hint at it, but they never explain
it completely.*
Yes, and you also accomplish something by showing the attitude of
the other people toward that character. You make whatever they do
as important to the story. Because Barthelmess was a pariah when
he came in there. But he had a beautiful wife, and it was kinda fun
fussing around with the fact that maybe Cary Grant – well, you
knew that he had an affair with the girl before, didn't you?

How did you go about conveying that?
Well, now, we were making a scene, and Rita Hayworth was
frightened. She had some lines to read, and she came through the
doorway so fast up to where Cary Grant was at a desk that I said,
'Hey, hey, wait a minute. This is wrong. Do it the opposite way.
Come in, close the door behind you, and lean back and look at him.'
And I said, 'What are you thinking about?' She said, 'Well, he's
looking at me. I'm a little self-conscious.' 'OK, say, "Do you like my
hair this way?"' Now, what does that tell you? You know that
they've been together. Then she came across and she kissed him. She

33 *Only Angels Have Wings*: Rita Hayworth with Richard Barthelmess.

34 *Only Angels Have Wings*: Hawks shooting a scene with Thomas
Mitchell and Jean Arthur.

didn't do much, and I said, 'Wait a minute, do a good job of it. And then say, "I don't know whether you should have done that." In other words, make it apparent that you did it, but blame *him*.' He said to her, 'I see you still use the same old goo.' OK, now, you can make up your own mind as to what they were, can't you? You know that they slept together. You know everything. So you've got something. You've got a man coming in with a new wife, so you expect something of it. You don't necessarily have to *do* anything. We didn't do anything with it. In *Red River*, Monty Clift and John Ireland tried out guns together, and people talked about 'em – 'If those two ever tangled . . .' You always expected a fight. I never made a fight with 'em.

The screenwriter Jules Furthman, who worked with you several times [*on* Come and Get It, Only Angels Have Wings, The Outlaw, To Have and Have Not, The Big Sleep, *and* Rio Bravo, *as well as on* Underworld], *is sort of a mysterious figure. It's hard to know exactly what he contributed to your work.*

A kind of cynicism, an idea of doing different things. For instance, when we were doing *To Have and Have Not,* he wrote an introduction to Bacall: she was a stranger in a strange land, and her purse was stolen. He said, 'What do you think of it?' I said, 'Jules, I don't like it at all – if there's anything that gives me a hard-on, it's a girl who gets her purse stolen . . .' 'Jesus, that's a great scene, you son of a bitch!' he said. And he went off, and he wrote a scene where *she* stole the purse. Well, that was Furthman. He had a great ability to think of new ways of doing things. Von Sternberg could use Furthman because of the fact that he did things differently. And Fleming could use him; I could use him. We were about the only people who could put up with the son of a bitch. Everybody hated him. He was such a mean guy that we thought he was just great. He was bright, and he was short. He'd say 'You stupid guy' to somebody who wasn't as smart as him. He needed help, but when he got help he was awful good.

One of the best-known lines in American film is from To Have and Have Not: *'You don't have to do anything. Not a thing . . . Oh, maybe, just whistle.' Who was responsible – Faulkner, Furthman, Hawks, or did it come out of a rehearsal?*

Oh, I was making a test of Bacall, so I wrote the scene just for the test, and it went over so well we had an awful time trying to put it into the picture. Faulkner was the one who found a place to put it. He said, 'If we put those people in a hotel corridor where nobody else is around, then I think we can make that scene work.' So we did it. I wrote the line, but he wrote the stuff that led up to it.

Do you remember the reason you decided not to have Harry Morgan missing one arm in To Have and Have Not, *as he was in the book?*

A very simple reason: I don't know how to do a one-armed man. I could put a hook on him like I did with Eddie Robinson in *Tiger Shark*, but every time I got Eddie in a scene I had to arrange it so you can't see that it was an extension on his arm. The only good thing about the one-arm thing [in Hemingway's novel *To Have and Have Not*] was that the girl made that one arm an asset. She received the one arm and got a physical kick out of it. He poked it in her. That was a great relationship – a girl that would do that. So that gave us a lot of ideas about some relationship.

There are certain lines that recur in your films. Specifically, lines like, 'I'm hard to get, all you have to do is ask me,' and 'Do you think you're good enough?' Why do you use them so often?

Well, 'I'm hard to get, all you have to do is ask me' – it just happens that I like that frankness and honesty. And if I like the girl, the character, well enough, I say, 'Tell 'em that.' You can tell 'em a variation, but they'll always end up by saying, 'I'm hard to get, all you have to do is ask me.' I used it in *Only Angels Have Wings*. And I used it for Bacall. Now, 'Are you good enough?' – that's one of the most common questions that men ask one another. So it's only natural to do it. I don't know any other way to phrase it. If you can think of a way, tell me, and I'll use it in the next picture.

16

His Girl Friday

How did you get the idea to change the sex of the Hildy Johnson character when you adapted The Front Page *into* His Girl Friday?

We were having dinner one night at the house, six or eight people, and we were talking about dialogue. I said that the finest modern dialogue in the world came from Hecht and MacArthur. After dinner we went in, and I had two copies of their play *The Front Page*. There was a girl there who was pretty good, and I said, 'Read the reporter's part, and I'll read the editor's part.' And in the middle of it, I said, 'My Lord, it's better with a girl reading it than the way it was!' See, *The Front Page* was intended as a love affair between two men. I mean, they *loved* each other. There's no doubt about it. And it was a lot easier for me to make a love story with a man and a girl and make some better scenes. It required so little change in dialogue that it was just simple. I tried Gene Fowler and a couple of other people, and they said they wouldn't have anything to do with such nonsense. So I called Hecht up in New York, and I said, 'What do you think about changing Hildy Johnson and making her a girl?' He said, 'I wish we'd thought of that.' And he said, 'I'm stuck on a story, if you'll help me I'll come out there and help you.' So he came out, and I helped him with his story and he helped me. I went in to Harry Cohn, and I said, 'I'm ready to make a picture.' He said, 'What?' I said, 'A remake of *Front Page*.' 'Oh,' he said, 'you don't want to do that.' I said, 'OK.' I got up, and he said, 'Where are you going? Now, well, wait a minute, wait a minute. You must have a good idea.' I said, 'I think I have.' He said, 'Well, wouldn't [Walter] Winchell be good as the editor and Cary Grant as the reporter?' 'Well, you're half right,' I said. 'Cary Grant would make a good editor, and a girl could be the reporter.' And he said, 'Oh, you're nuts.' I said, 'Harry, I'm going to go. I've had enough. If you don't

35 *His Girl Friday*: Rosalind Russell (as Hildy Johnson) with fellow members of the press.

36 *His Girl Friday*: Two men and a girl – Ralph Bellamy, Cary Grant and Rosalind Russell.

like the idea, then I don't want to make it for you.' He said, 'Wait a minute, wait a minute, wait a minute. I know enough not to try and tell you how to make pictures.' And we made it, and it made a lot of money.

In His Girl Friday *the dialogue was much faster than normal. And the actors were stepping on each other's lines throughout the film. How did you make that work?*
If you'll ever listen to some people who are talking, especially in a scene of any excitement, they all talk at the same time. All it needs is a little extra work on the dialogue. You put a few words in front of somebody's speech and put a few words at the end, and they can overlap it. It gives you a sense of speed that actually doesn't exist. And then you make the people talk a little faster. I've done that through many pictures, but we started it in this picture. [Although Hawks used rapid dialogue in *Twentieth Century*, it was not pushed as far as in *His Girl Friday*, which has had more of an impact on other film-makers.] Everybody said that the original *Front Page* [1931, directed by Lewis Milestone and produced by Howard Hughes] was the fastest picture that was ever made. So I told Hecht and MacArthur what I was going to do. We were all talking, the three of us at the same time, and I said, 'Just the way we're talking now.' They said that was a good idea. I said, 'I'd like to show them that the first picture was not as fast.' We had an interesting thing during the making of it – the newspapermen, who looked on the story of *Front Page* as a sort of Bible, were rather horrified at the idea of changing the reporter into a girl. We arranged a showing to the newspapermen, and we had the screen split in two parts. We ran the one picture on one and the other picture on the other, and they said, 'My God, your picture's so much faster than the other!'

17

Camerawork

I try to tell my story as simply as possible, with the camera at eye level. I just imagine the way the story should be told, and I do it. If it's a scene that I don't want anybody to monkey with or cut, I don't give them any way to cut it. If I think that it's a little too long and the actors are dawdling and I want to cut some of it out, I make two angles so that I can cut it. That's about all I can say about it. I like to tell it with a simple scene. I don't want you to be conscious that this is dramatic, because it throws it all off. People ask me why I had the shot in *El Dorado* of the man falling into the camera. Well, they don't know that I didn't have any set to work with; I *had* to do it that way. I like the scene in *El Dorado* where Wayne and the girl said goodbye in the door and he rode off amongst the cactus as the sun was going down. When I got down there I said, 'Build me a set with a big doorway.' We watched the sun go down, picked out a spot, staked it in the ground, set up the camera, and waited for a good sunset. I went and made it in ten minutes and walked away. It looked beautiful on the screen.

Do you ever use a storyboard?
Never heard of one.

What do you think of a director like Hitchcock, who has all the camera angles worked out in the office before he starts shooting?
I think he's great. I couldn't do it the way he does it, and he couldn't do it the way I do or the way Capra does. He has to see it alone, go it alone, and it comes out all right because he's good at it.

What kind of relationship do you find best to have with your cameraman?
There's a lot of cooperation with a good cameraman, and I've been

fortunate in having good ones. Some of them get very tired working in normal stuff, they relax, and then you pep them up and get them to take chances. I tell them, 'If you make two good scenes for me, you can make two mediocre ones and one bad one.' All I'm interested in is the good one. So they go ahead and take chances, and their work shows it. Because you people pass up the bad scenes, but you really appreciate the good one.

One especially good scene was in Ball of Fire, *when Gregg Toland did a close-up of Barbara Stanwyck with everything in darkness except her eyes.*
He was a hell of a cameraman. We had a marvellous scene where Cooper had to come in to say something to the girl. She was in bed, you couldn't see her face, you could just see her eyes. I said to Toland, 'How the hell can I do that? How can I light her eyes without lighting her face?' And he said, 'Well, have her do it in blackface.' So the next day I saw her and said, 'Barbara, tomorrow don't bother making up. I want you to play in blackface.' She said, 'What the hell kind of scene is that?' Oh, God, it was a good scene.

Quite often you have your action sequences take place at night. Is that done for a specific purpose, such as heightening the suspense?
Action scenes are much more dramatic if they're shot at night. You're able to light the set so the audience sees what you want them to see. You go out in bright sunlight and shoot – oh, there's so many things for your eye to follow, and it's hard to get away with it. I don't know, it's just something that I've always done.

Would you talk about your use of colour?
When we were making *Red River*, we discussed whether to use colour or not. At that time colour wasn't very good. It had a kind of garish look to it. I didn't like it, and we were trying to get a feeling of the period, so we made *Red River* in black-and-white. Some things I think go well in black-and-white; they give you a feeling of being *older*. Now colour is better, and it'd be pretty hard for me to make a picture without colour. I think I enjoy it now. We've learned how to handle it, to control it, to print it. The colour is faster, so we can use

it just as if we were using black-and-white; it doesn't jump at us. We can use all the fall colours, ambers and muted colours, and come out with a very good-looking picture. In *El Dorado*, I noticed that the Remington paintings always had a great slash of light across the street coming out of the saloon door. So I said to the cameraman [Harold Rosson], 'How do we get this?' He said, 'Use yellow light, but don't walk your people through it – they'll look like they had yellow jaundice or something.' He used back light on them, and it was a very mellow, pleasant look. We used it in the last picture [*Rio Lobo*].

You almost never use extreme close shots. Why?
I use them wherever I think you need them for emphasis. But I get awful sick of the trend in television where it's all made in close shots. And some of the best scenes that you make are in long shot. I learned that from Jack Ford. Peter Bogdanovich has done that very successfully in *The Last Picture Show*, but he sat on my set for two and a half years and on Ford's for two and a half years, so he learned a few things.

How did you get the idea in Red River *to start the cattle drive with all those close-ups, maybe twenty cowboys in a row? It's very unusual, especially for you.*
One of the toughest things about doing a story where you're gonna have eight or ten people and you're gonna carry them all the way through is, how do you introduce them? Well, the quicker that you can get up to a close-up and show them, and the more varied their costumes are, the more chance that people are gonna recognize who it is. So I started right in the beginning by making close-ups of these fellows, and it made a sort of a feeling that the music carried it along. It gave us a good start for the cattle drive. Whenever I made a western, I had Joe De Yong, who was a protégé of Charles Russell, draw sketches of every character. I don't know whether you happen to remember that in *Red River* one cowboy had a derby hat on. They all had different kinds of hats – cavalry hats, forage hats – so you could tell who the hell the people were. I gave Montgomery Clift my hat, which Gary Cooper gave to me. To make it look

weatherbeaten, Coop used to take it out every night and water it. Spiders built nests in it. It looked great.

Do you feel that fancy camerawork detracts from a story?
Well, the fellow who handles the camera better than anybody else, [Henry] Hathaway, has never made any particularly great pictures. The mechanical thing doesn't seem to make any difference. Back in the earlier days Woody Van Dyke used to make some of the great pictures, things with Bill Powell and Myrna Loy and a bunch of things like that. He just set the camera up and shot. Absolutely no composition, no movement, nothing at all, just put the camera up and shot. They'd lay out his work for him, he'd be through by one o'clock and go home. He made good pictures.

37 *Ball of Fire*: Gary Cooper and Barbara Stanwyck.

38 *Ball of Fire*: Barbara Stanwyck teaching the professors how to dance.

18

Samuel Goldwyn

One mystery which has never been explained is why William Wyler replaced you as director on the Samuel Goldwyn film Come and Get It.

Goldwyn really tried like hell to make good pictures, but we didn't get along too well. He didn't think a director should write. He was crazy about writers, and he really tried to get the finest authors he could get ahold of. He got Edna Ferber's story because Edna Ferber was supposed to be a good writer, and there were a great many things that I didn't like about the story. Goldwyn was going to the hospital, and he asked me to make it. He said, 'You're in charge.' So I changed the little lame girl who sang so badly that the woodsmen hooted at her to a lusty wench, you know, and when he came back I had about a week more of work to do. He saw what I had shot, and it was a shock to him. He bought a story, and he didn't get it. He cast a girl in it, and the girl wasn't used – I used Frances Farmer, who was getting seventy-five dollars a week, for most of it. He told me a director shouldn't write, and I wasn't very polite with my answer. So Willy Wyler was put on, and Wyler photographed six hundred feet of the film, and Goldwyn gave him credit for being co-director. [Wyler has said that Goldwyn wanted to remove Hawks's name from the picture entirely; Wyler told Goldwyn that Hawks deserved sole directing credit, and Goldwyn then decided on the joint credit.]

Why did you do A Song Is Born, *the musical remake of* Ball of Fire? Because I got $25,000 a week, that's why. Goldwyn pestered me and pestered me. He said, 'There's some way to do it.' I came up with a way, then he wouldn't let me do anything. I think Goldwyn realized that he'd made a silly contract with me, that he'd made a fool of

39 *A Song Is Born*: 'I never thought anything in that picture was funny' –
Virginia Mayo, Danny Kaye and Steve Cochran.

40 *A Song Is Born*: Some of the best musical talent in America – Benny
Goodman with clarinet (back to camera), Louis (Satchmo) Armstrong,
Lionel Hampton with vibraphone, and Tommy Dorsey with trombone
(back to camera).

himself, and he was so mad at having made it that he wanted to try and gum things up. He certainly did. And it wasn't easy. Danny Kaye had always done his wife's material. He'd separated from his wife, and he was a basket case, stopping work to see a psychiatrist twice a day. Now you can imagine working with that. He was about as funny as a crutch. It was an altogether horrible experience. I've never seen the picture.

Did Goldwyn come on the set and try to interfere with you?
Yeah, and I'd insult him as much as I could. I'd say, 'You're spilling stuff on your tie again, Sam.'

A Song Is Born *is not as good as the original, by far, but I thought the last part worked better.*
I thought it did too.

It was more suspenseful and funny at the same time.
I never thought anything in that picture was funny.

What did you think of Virginia Mayo?
Pathetic.

She was the wrong girl in that film. She didn't have what Barbara Stanwyck had. And she didn't have a flair for comedy.
In the first place, Sam Goldwyn told me if I'd do the picture, he promised me I didn't have to have Virginia Mayo. Then we not only had to take Virginia Mayo, but he had her run *Ball of Fire* about twenty times and rehearse with somebody else to play Stanwyck's scenes. She's not Stanwyck, I'll tell you that. So he just loaded the thing up so that there was no chance of making a good scene.

There were so many musicians in the film, but they were not utilized.
Well, we'd get something all ready, and then I'd get orders to do a different thing.

The best talent in America was there, really. Everybody was there –
Tommy Dorsey, Louis Armstrong, Benny Goodman, Lionel
Hampton . . .
Oh, so many of them were great. One of the things they [the studio]
said was, 'Look, now, don't get the Negroes and the white musicians
too close together.' And I said, 'Get yourself another director, will
you? I'm not going to pay any attention to that. To hell with you. As
far as I'm concerned, the Negroes belong in music because they're
part of this kind of music.' Well, the whole thing was unfortunate.
Only one good thing happened. Satchmo and I became such good
friends. I was over in Africa making a picture once, and I got a
strange fever. I went over to the nursing home – they didn't have
hospitals, they had nursing homes – for a couple of days, and
Satchmo was touring over there, and he heard I was there. He came
up to the hospital to see me, and that made me a hero with all of the
Negroes in Africa. I got a lot more respect from the Negroes after
that.

Do you have any amusing stories of working with Sam Goldwyn?
I remember one. He brought in a very good-looking girl, a writer,
and he said, 'I want you two to cohabit very closely.' I said, 'I'd be
glad to do that.' Damn good-looking girl.

19

Sergeant York

41 *Sergeant York*: Gary Cooper – the moral crisis of a pacifist who goes to war and becomes a war hero.

Hal Wallis [Warner Brothers' head of production] gave me the script and said, 'If you don't do this, we're gonna make a B-picture out of it.' I said, 'That's a great way to tell somebody . . .' When I read it, I said to tell him it's about as bad as he indicated it was. And I went in to see Jesse Lasky [the producer], who needed a shave and had the shakes, and I said, 'Look, close your door, and tell the secretary no calls, and tell me why the hell you bought this story.' He gave me my first good job, and I knew he was a great story mind. And he told me an entirely different story from the script. So I said, 'Jesse, I'll make the picture if it's OK with you that I just do the story you told me.' 'Oh, Christ,' he said, 'sure.' And I said, 'I'll get Cooper.' He said,

42 *Sergeant York*: The camaraderie of the group.

43 *Sergeant York*: Shooting the trenches.

'You can't get him. I tried to.' So I went back, and I called Cooper, and I said, 'I just talked to Lasky. Didn't he give you your first job?' Coop said yes. 'Well,' I said, 'he's broke, he's got the shakes, he needs a shave, and he's got a story that I don't think would hurt you to do, or me.' He said, 'I'll come over and talk to you.' And he came over, and he said, 'Where's that new gun of yours?' He didn't want to talk about anything. Finally I said, 'Look, Coop, we have to talk about this.' He said, 'What the hell is there to talk about? You know we're gonna do it.' So I said, 'Well, come with me, and if I say "Isn't that right, Mr Cooper?" you say, "Yup."' So we went over and saw Hal Wallis, and I said, 'We'll do the picture for you if you stay out of our way and don't interfere at all. Isn't that right, Mr Cooper?' 'Yup.' 'We're gonna change the plot, the story around. Isn't that right, Mr Cooper?' 'Yup.' 'I'm gonna use Johnny Huston as a writer.' Well, they had to say yes, and we started to work on it. We just kept about three days ahead of Johnny Huston writing. I ran into Warner one day, and I said, 'Even if you can't come down and talk to me, can't you write me a note and say what you think, it's lousy or good?' He said, 'I haven't seen it.' So I said, 'Well, I'm gonna sit on the set and not do a goddam take until you go and look at it.' He came running back and said, 'Jesus Christ, that's the greatest film I've ever seen. What do you want?' I said, 'I just want the same thing as we've got – stay away and don't bother us. But look at the film.' So we made it, and I cut it, and he sent it right to the negative cutter – the first time he ever did that – and I said, 'There's work I want to do on it.' He said, 'You're not gonna spoil this.' He sent it off. Oh, Warner was fine. He didn't bother you making a movie. Johnny Huston did such a good script for me that I suggested to Warner that they make him a director. Johnny came back and said, 'What should I write?' And I said, 'Don't write anything. It's hard enough to direct your first picture. There's a story that Warners owns that I've always been going to do called *The Maltese Falcon*.' He came back again and said, 'It's been made twice,' and I said, 'It's *never* been made. Always some idiot thought he could write better than Dashiell Hammett. You go and make *Maltese Falcon* exactly the way Hammett wrote it, use the dialogue, don't change a goddam thing, and you'll have a hell of a picture.'

And he and I were up against each other for an Academy Award at the end of the year. [It was Hawks's only Oscar nomination. The following question was asked in 1974, the year before he received his honorary Oscar.]

Does it bother you that you've never won an Oscar?
Not a bit. I don't agree with most of the Oscar selections, so that's probably why it doesn't bother me.

20

Air Force

Air Force is a film which hasn't been talked about much by critics or, for some reason, in your interviews, but it's a fine film, very authentic-looking.

I've been flying all my life. I made it because I knew [Major] General [Henry H.] Arnold, the head of the Air Force [actually, at that time, the US Army Air Forces], since he was a captain. He asked me to make a film for him. Christ, he even made me a general for a week. I was doing a bunch of things for him, and the first general with a higher rank that I ran into, I called Arnold's office and said, 'Hap, I'm sitting next to a guy who has three stars on his shoulder. He doesn't want to do what I want to do. I'm not a general any more, will you tell him to do what I want him to do?' The general said, 'Boy, it didn't take you too long to settle that!' I told Hap, 'I don't want to be a general – as a civilian I can ask for anything.' *Air Force* is actually a true story. The whole story is based on complete fact. All we did was trim it up and add some things and put some characters in it. But it was one of the hardest stories to tell. Arnold sent us people who were intimately connected with that phase, and we recorded what they told us. Then Dudley Nichols and I had the job of deciding what we were gonna use and what we weren't gonna use. We got a great big board. We got all kinds of baggage tags – red, yellow, blue – and scenes that we had taken from the history of that flight, that we knew we had to use, we'd say, 'Put 'em on red.' And we hung those up on the board. Then little love scenes we made another colour. And we'd tack up other things. Then we'd look at 'em to see how the colours were mixed up, and we switched 'em around. And, of course, we got a great deal of help from the Air Force itself.

44 *Air Force*: The camaraderie of the group.

45 *Air Force*: John Garfield – just one of the crew.

Did they tell you how to make the film, or was it left up to you?
That was left up to me, because I knew Arnold. [Air Force General]
Curt[is] Le May wanted me to do the story that they made [in 1955]
about the long-range bombers, *Strategic Air Command*. And when
a bunch of people started telling me what kinds of things I could do
and what I can't do, I said, 'I don't want to do it.'

It's interesting that John Garfield is in Air Force, *because he was
quite a big star at the time, and yet he doesn't really have the leading
role. Everybody has the same size part. How did that happen?*
He came around and said he wanted to be in it. And I said, 'I haven't
got much for you, you're just gonna be one of the crew.' He said,
'That's all I want to be.' And as a matter of fact, he's about the only
well-known actor in it. Well, Harry Carey –

He was terrific in that picture.
Oh, he was great. I was going back to Washington to see Arnold. In
New York, after I got tickets to go to Washington, there was a little
general who had brought two heavy bags. He was late, I was late,
and I said, 'Gotta hurry, general, I'll take one of your bags for you.'
We got on the train, and I found out he was the head of all
transportation. I said, 'I'm going down to see Hap Arnold. I'm
going to make a movie about that transport plane.' He said, 'Can I
help you?' and he came back with his crew chief, a sergeant, who
was in another part of the train. That was Harry Carey.

So you took the character from a living person.
The moment this general and the sergeant relaxed and had a drink,
they talked. And the sergeant would tell me stories about the general
getting all mixed up, you know, and all kinds of things like that. So I
had the character right then and there. And Dudley wrote it.

*Several of the younger actors in the film became rather well-known
later, Arthur Kennedy, Gig Young –*
I know it. There was that marvellous comic in it, George Tobias.
Everybody wanted to work in it, so it was easy. I had no troubles at
all with them. It took time to do the formation flying and the

backgrounds and things to get ready for it. But once we got started it didn't take too long.

How about the landing at Pearl Harbor?
It was a lot of work, because we had to leave a good place to land and put all the debris on the side. We didn't do that in Hawaii; we did that down in Florida. And I don't imagine that anybody could tell that it was done in Hawaii or Florida.

Did you have any conflicts with the studio on Air Force?
I did with Hal Wallis. I had a very bad cold and was out. Jack Warner called me and said, 'Hey, when are you coming back? This stuff they're shooting doesn't look like the same bunch of people.' I said, 'When's that guy going to get through wasting your money?' I went back, and there wasn't anything that they'd made that I could use. It was lousy. You thought that they were going to sing 'The Star-Spangled Banner' every time they were going to make a scene. And when I was cutting the end of the picture, Wallis wanted to get back to show it to General Arnold. He grabbed it and went back before I was able to get the end of it right.

The ending, the obliteration of the Japanese fleet, goes on so long that it seems like the film is piling it on excessively.
That wasn't my fault. We took thousands of feet of film of miniatures and all those things. They just saw the first cut; they released the first assembly. Nothing I could do. There was too much of it. Wallis went to Washington, and Arnold said, 'Where's Howard? We'll wait to look at it until he gets here.' Wallis is a good producer, but I had trouble with him. He stopped my cheque. I went to the window to get my cheque, and it wasn't there. I called my lawyer and said, 'I want to get away from Warner Brothers, is this sufficient excuse?' And he said, 'Take a witness with you, and if they refuse it again, your contract's broken.' So I took a witness, and two or three days later, I went in to see Wallis, and I said, 'Thank you for breaking my contract.' He said, 'What do you mean?' 'I went to get my cheque, and it wasn't there.' 'Oh, it was there.' I said, 'I *told* you it wasn't there.' He said, 'It *was* there.' I went over and

locked the door, and I said, 'Now, you son of a bitch, say it again.' And he started running around the room, and I put one hand in my pocket, and I said, 'I can do it with one hand.' So he sued me, and the judge threw it out of court. Warner hired me back for a lot more money on a different contract. I never had any trouble with Jack. Every picture I made with him made money.

21

Ernest Hemingway

A couple of years ago you were going to direct a film about the friendship of Hemingway and Robert Capa, the news photographer. Are you still working on that?
Well, I tell you, when you make a picture about real people, and their names are used, you have more trouble . . . in making *Sergeant York* we had to get twenty releases – every member of his squad in the Army, his lieutenant, his captain, his major, anybody that we mentioned we had to get releases. I think the story of getting the releases, where we found the various people and how we paid them off, was almost better than *Sergeant York*. I'm too goddam lazy, and I've got to have too much fun to run around getting releases. The head of one of the big companies, who wants me to make it, I told him I'd make the story if he'd get the releases. He said, 'I didn't know it was that much trouble.' You've got Hemingway's family to contend with, his ex-wives – oh, Christ! So for the moment it's stymied. I don't know whether to do it or not. I don't know who the hell to do it with. It must be George C. Scott.

World War II was an interesting period in Hemingway's life. From reading about it, it seems he was a little unbalanced. He was doing a lot of bizarre things, getting into the war even though he was a correspondent, blowing up pillboxes . . .
I wouldn't say it was in *that* period; he had done that all his life. What the hell, he was mixed up in the Spanish War long before that. I remember one funny thing – Capa went over with the first wave that went through the water at Anzio beachhead. He made those marvellous pictures of everything shaking. Ernest got over by flying over three or four days later. He got mixed up in some way, and Capa found him shot in the leg or something. Capa left him for

about three hours and went on to get his camera so he could get a picture of Ernest's leg.

What kind of a guy was Capa?
He was ebullient. He was a great photographer. He was Hungarian. He was crazy as a bedbug. You see, the story of one man gets kind of boring, but the story of a friendship is something that lets you make better scenes. Capa was going out in Paris with a very good-looking Eurasian model, but he had a hell of a time every time he visited her place because the girl had a great big boxer dog that didn't like Capa. Ernest came over, and after a few drinks he told Capa he had a sleeping pill that was a suppository. So Ernest poked it in the dog. Capa got brave and stayed, and he woke up in the morning, and the dog was going '*Grrr*' right in his face. And I remember Hemingway's new wife [Mary Welsh] one time stopping Capa from throwing knives at Ernest when Ernest was standing with his arms out in front of a door and both were drunk. And all kinds of crazy things they used to do. Nobody else can do 'em, they don't know the things, because I've seen them happen.

Would it be a comedy?
Well, I don't know. Especially in the last ten or twelve years, every time I can get some comedy into a scene, I'll do it. You can call it a comedy if you want to. It isn't an outright comedy, but I would much rather tell these things than something serious. Hemingway was . . . we were good friends. He interested me. Strange guy.

To Have and Have Not *doesn't have much to do with Hemingway's novel.*
There wasn't *anything* in the picture that was in the book. Hemingway and I were fishing down in Key West, and I was trying to get him to write for movies. He said, 'No, I'm top where I am. I don't want to go out to Hollywood. I don't like it. And I wouldn't know what to do.' I said, 'You don't have to come to Hollywood. We can go fishing or hunting. We can meet here, Sun Valley, Africa, any place you want, and write a story.' 'Oh,' he said, 'I'd rather not.' I said, 'Look, you're broke all the time. Why the deuce don't you

46 *To Have and Have Not*: Walter Brennan, Lauren Bacall and
Humphrey Bogart.

make some money? Anything you write you can make into a movie.
I can make a movie out of the worst thing you ever wrote.' He said,
'What's the worst thing I ever wrote?' I said, 'That piece of junk
called *To Have and Have Not*.' 'I needed money,' he said. I said,
'Well, I knew that. At least I had to guess it.' He said, 'You can't
make a picture out of that.' And I said, 'No, but the two leading
characters were marvellous in their relationship with each other.
What about if we told how they met?' So just for fun for two weeks
while we were hunting dove and quail and duck, and fishing, we
worked on it and tried to figure out what kind of a picture we could
make. He'd sold the picture rights for $10,000, and I paid the guy
[Howard Hughes] $80,000 for the story. And I sold it to Warner
Brothers for half the profit of the picture and got well paid besides.
When I saw Ernest in Paris later, I said, 'Ernest, you got $10,000, the
other guy got $80,000, I got about $1,200,000 out of it.' He got so
mad he wouldn't talk to me for six months.

You were planning a film of The Sun Also Rises *for a while.*
Yeah, I bought it fifteen years before I sold it to some poor guy
[Darryl Zanuck, who filmed it in 1957 with Henry King directing].

*It's been said that the reason you didn't make it was that you
couldn't decide how to turn it into a comedy.*
Oh, no. I thought it was hard to do. It was about a fellow who
was impotent. [Hawks misunderstood Jake Barnes's problem. As
Hemingway explained in A. E. Hotchner's *Papa Hemingway*, the
character had his penis shot off in the war but not his testicles, 'And
that was very important to the kind of man he was. His testicles
were intact. That was all he had, but this made him capable of
feeling everything a normal man feels but not able to do anything
about it. That the wound was a physical wound, and not a
psychological wound, was the vital thing' (p. 49).] Censors wouldn't
allow you to do the thing at that time. I did my best to try and figure
out a way, but I never could figure it out. Zanuck paid through the
nose for it, then six months later he called me up and said, 'Howard,
how were you gonna make that?' I said, 'Darryl, I'll be glad to tell
you for $100,000.'

I read an interview with you in the London Times *in which you said
that when Hemingway committed suicide you lost your respect for
him. Is that the way you feel about it?*
Yeah. I don't like suicide.

*But wasn't he so sick that he was really a physical wreck and
mentally messed up?*
I never heard anything about that. I heard he was impotent.

So you think he lost his will power?
Well, there's no telling. You can't figure. Vic Fleming and I were
living together when a fellow left one night, and Vic said, 'Hey, you
know, he was talking about committing suicide. I think the son of a
bitch is gonna do it.' I said, 'Do you think so?' 'Yeah,' he said, 'let's
go over and find out.' We went over to the fellow's house, and he
was out on the floor, and the gas was on. We opened the windows,

we turned off the gas. It was in the middle of winter. We got a big bucket of ice water and threw it over him and got a bottle of Scotch and let him soak there.

The Hawksian Woman

47 Frances Farmer in *Come and Get It* – 'The best actress I ever worked with.'

I've been accused of promoting Women's Lib, and I've denied it, emphatically. It just happens that kind of a woman is attractive to me. I merely am doing somebody that I like. And I've seen so many pictures where the hero gets in the moonlight and says silly things to a girl, I'd reverse it and let the girl do the chasing around, you know, and it works out pretty well. Anyway, I know that a little better than I do that other stuff. I'd much rather work with a character like that than with some little Puritan violet. I think that it's pretty apparent the kind of people that we like, that you see on the screen. I like Carole Lombard, I like Rita Hayworth, I like Angie Dickinson. I could keep on naming dozens of them. They're the kind of stars that people like. As long as the people like those characters, I'm going to keep on doing them.

Which of the women in your films was your personal favourite?
I don't think there's any doubt that Frances Farmer was the best actress I ever worked with. She was in *Come and Get It*. She was just a kid who came in to audition for another part. I said, 'You ought to play the lead,' and she said, 'Let me do it.' So I paid off the star that Goldwyn had signed and put this kid in, and I thought she did an amazing piece of work. She was probably one of the cleanest, simplest, hardest-working persons I ever knew. She came a couple of times to my boat wearing her sweatshirt and her dungarees and carrying a toothbrush in her pocket. She had no phoniness about her at all. She studied under a very fine teacher in Washington. When I told her the part I said, 'I want to make a test.' She played the mother and daughter roles in the picture, and she tried to do the mother by make-up, you know, things like that, and she failed. She was one of the first persons to see it. She said, 'Does that mean I'm out?' And I said, 'Hell, no, you've got the part. I'll meet you tonight about eight o'clock. Where do you live?' And she told me. I said, 'I can't find that; I'll meet you up on such-and-such a corner.' We went to all kinds of beer joints, little places around town, looking for a woman of her type. We finally found a marvellous one, and I said, 'Now, you do something. You come in here every night for two weeks. You get picked up; what'll probably happen is some guy will try to feel your leg. You're a strong girl; you can handle yourself.

Whoever does it, talk to him, be that woman, with her mannerisms and everything. And then we'll make a test.' She was just fabulous. She was a blonde, a natural, but she just used a dark wig; that's all she put on. No change in make-up, just her face changed. Her whole attitude changed, her whole method of talking. And she just really . . . the very first day I remember her working with Eddie Arnold, who was a real old trouper, and she said, 'If you'd only speak that line a little quicker I could keep this thing going.' And he looked at her, and he spoke it quicker, and the scene was better. He said, 'Hey, look, she's pretty good.' I said, 'She's so good that you'd better get right to work or she's going to take it and walk off with it.' If it hadn't been for personal things that happened to her [she was incarcerated in a mental hospital and was given a lobotomy], she'd have gone on and been a very big star. She just went to pieces.

One good actress I've heard you weren't pleased with was Jean Arthur, in Only Angels Have Wings. *Why was that?*
She didn't fit into the kind of girl that I liked. I thought she was good, but she'd simply say, 'I can't do that kind of stuff.' She was afraid to try anything on the spur of the moment. When the picture was over I said, 'Jean, I think you're the only person I've ever worked with that I don't think I helped a bit. Some day you will see in a picture what I wanted you to play.' Then one time I came home, and there was a car in the driveway. Jean was in the back seat. She said, 'I saw *To Have and Have Not.* I wish I'd done what you'd asked me to do. If you ever make another picture with me, I'll promise to do any goddam thing you want to do. If a kid can come in and do that kind of stuff, I certainly could do it.' I said, 'I know you could.'

Tell me about how you found Lauren Bacall.
Bacall had about four months of the toughest kind of training before we put her in *To Have and Have Not.* I saw a picture of Bacall in a magazine [*Harper's Bazaar*], and my secretary made a mistake and brought her out here from New York. All I wanted to do was find out her background, whether she'd studied, whether she'd played any scenes, what she'd done. Instead of that, she arrived. All of a

48 Hawks with Jean Arthur – 'The only person I've ever worked with that I don't think I helped a bit.'

sudden this kid appeared in a gabardine skirt and a sweater. She was only nineteen. And, well, she talked in a little high nasal voice. But she was so eager, she wanted to work and everything, that I couldn't send her home; I had to give her some kind of a chance. I said to the secretary, 'Look, get her a car, send her around to some studios, and I'll send her back home.' But she didn't want to go to the studios; she wanted to start to work. And I had to tell her that we made pictures about a fairly sophisticated girl, that the kind of girls I like in a movie didn't have little high nasal voices. I said, 'You just can't possibly read any of the lines that we write.' Didn't bother her, she said, 'What do I do to change my voice?' I said, 'I don't know, but I can tell you what the best actor I ever worked with, Walter Huston [who starred in *The Criminal Code* for Hawks], told me how he got the voice that he did.' You may remember that the first time he ever sang in his life, he made a record, and it sold a million copies – 'September Song'. He could do anything with his voice. Anyway, I told her, and she disappeared for three weeks.

What did you tell her to do?
I'd have to write it out for you. It'd take a long time. [In her 1979 autobiography, *By Myself*, Bacall explained, 'He wanted me to drive into the hills, find some quiet spot, and read aloud. He felt it most important to keep the voice in a low register. Mine started off low, but what Howard didn't like and explained to me was, "If you notice, Betty, when a woman gets excited or emotional she tends to raise her voice. Now, there is nothing more unattractive than screeching. I want you to train your voice in such a way that even if you have a scene like that your voice will remain low." I found a spot on Mulholland Drive and proceeded to read *The Robe* aloud, keeping my voice lower and louder than normal. If anyone had ever passed by, they would have found me a candidate for the asylum. Who sat on mountaintops in cars reading books aloud to the canyons? Who did? I did.'] I'd ask my secretary, 'Where's that girl?' 'Oh, she phones in and says that she's not ready, but she'll come in.' And in about three weeks she walked in and said, 'Hello, how are ya?' [deep voice]. She really worked. You had to give her credit. We used to have a party out at the house on Saturday night. While she

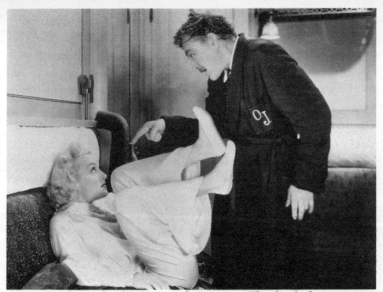

49 Carole Lombard in *Twentieth Century* – 'That kind of woman is attractive to me.'

50 Lauren Bacall in *To Have and Have Not* – a good illustration of Hawks's use of low-key lighting with the overhanging lamp as light source.

was waiting around, she came out, and when it was all over, she was standing there. I had to give her a ride home. And I said, 'Can't you get a ride yourself so that I can get tight and not have to drive you back?' She said, 'I don't do too well with men.' I said, 'What do you do, are you nice to 'em?' She said, 'Nice as I can be.' And I said, 'Maybe that's wrong. Why don't you try *not* being nice? Why don't you try to insult them?' So the next Saturday night she came over kind of like the cat who's eaten the canary and said, 'Well, I got a ride home.' I said, 'What happened?' and she said, 'Oh, I insulted the man.' 'What'd you say to him?' 'I asked him where he got his tie. He said, "What do you want to know for?" And I said, "So I can tell people not to go there."' 'Oh,' I said, 'who's the man?' She said, 'Clark Gable.' So I went over on Monday to Jules Furthman and said, 'Do you suppose we could make a girl who is insolent, as insolent as Bogart, who insults people, who grins when she does it, and people like it?' He said, 'Where are you going to find such a creature?' I said, 'I don't know, but we can try writing it.' He thought it was fun, and we started to write the character. I would try out the scenes on Bacall. She was working all the time. One of the things that I did with her was I gave her a really good scene, and when she came in I said, 'Do you know the scene?' She said, 'Yeah.' I said, 'Are you doing it pretty good?' She said, 'I think I'm doing it well.' I said, 'I changed my mind. I want a girl with a Spanish accent. Do a Spanish accent.' She said, 'I don't know how to do a Spanish accent.' I said, 'I didn't ask you whether you knew how or not, I said do it with a Spanish accent.' Well, she was so bad I was crying, I was laughing so hard. She said, 'OK, you son of a bitch!' I said, 'Stop on the way out; get fifty bucks from the secretary. I know what you're gonna do, you're gonna get somebody to teach you an accent.' She said, 'I am.' Next time she came in, she said she was ready to read it. And I said, 'I changed my mind. I want a Swede.' I never let her read the scene the way she'd worked on it. She did seven different languages. By the time she got through, you couldn't worry her about anything. She just would do anything. She got better and better, and finally I said, 'I'm gonna put her into the lead.' Everybody said, 'You're nuts.' But it worked out, and she became an instant star. And it was that quality of insolence. That hadn't

51 *To Have and Have Not*: Bogart and Bacall (with Marcel Dalio in between) – 'When two people are falling in love with each other, they're not tough to get along with.'

been seen. It *had*, but people didn't remember it. Because Dietrich came up to me, and I won't say what she called me, but she said, 'You know, that's me about twenty years ago.' And I said, 'I know it. And twenty years from now there'll be another one with the same attitude.'

Were Bacall and Humphrey Bogart easy to get along with on the set?
When two people are falling in love with each other, they're not tough to get along with, I can tell you that. Bogey was marvellous. I said, 'You've got to help,' and, of course, after a few days he really began to get interested in the girl. That made him help more. And it wasn't hard at all. She found out that people liked her and that it didn't hurt her. She just waltzed through that picture. Now, she wasn't smart enough to do it on the third picture [*Confidential Agent*] that she did, after she did two with me. She forgot everything I told her; she didn't have Bogey around to help her. I saw it, and I

was horrified. I said, 'Bogey, haven't you followed her in this thing?' He said no. You couldn't let her go. 'Betty,' I said, 'couldn't you remember what I told you?' 'I guess I forgot,' she said. Oh, God, she was awful. So after that, why, Bogey rehearsed her and kept her doing it until she got it. She had to keep practising for six to eight months to keep that low voice. Now it's perfectly natural. And the funny thing is that Bogey fell in love with the character she played, so she had to keep playing it the rest of her life.

23

Bogart and *The Big Sleep*

Bogey was one of the best actors I've ever worked with. He was a far cry from the actors today, who are a little bit on the dilettante side. There was Bogey with a homely face and everything, and people adored him. When I started to work with him I said, 'Why don't you ever smile?' 'Oh,' he said, 'I got a bum lip.' He had a lip that was badly cut up, and I think the nerves were cut. And I said, 'Well, the other night when we got drunk you certainly were smiling and laughing a lot.' He said, 'Do you think I can?' And I said, 'You'd better if you're gonna work with me.' He became so much more attractive when he smiled.

Did you have any trouble with him?
I had trouble the first day with Bogart. I think I grabbed him by the lapels and pushed his head up against the wall, and said, 'Look, Bogey. I tell you how to get tough, but don't get tough with me.' He said, 'I won't.' Everything was fine from that time on. He had a couple of drinks at lunch, and that's what caused it. Stopped that.

Don Siegel, who was working in the montage department at Warner Brothers when you were directing there, said that you were the only director he ever saw who knew how to handle Bogart. Because you seemed to make Bogart feel that he was part of the creative process of making the film as opposed to just being an actor in it. Was that true?
Yeah, I think that's true. He certainly could do anything that you asked him to do, and he also took criticism without a murmur. We'd start a sequence, and he'd turn around and say, 'What do you think of that?' And I'd say, 'Duller than hell.' He'd say, 'Well, what do you mean?' I'm thinking, for instance, about one scene in *The Big Sleep*.

52 *The Big Sleep*: Bogart and Bacall.

53 *The Big Sleep*: Bogart and Dorothy Malone ('A darn good-looking girl.')

We had a bookstore built on a street; we made Bogart going inside. We hadn't done the scene in the bookstore. I said, 'I don't know what the hell we're gonna do when we get inside. I've got a good girl in there, she's pretty strong, and *look* at you. If it's as dull as that, we're gonna have a couple of bad scenes. I think the only way to go in would be in a different character. Just so it would be fun when we got in.' 'Oh,' he said, 'what can you think of?' I said, 'I don't know, can you play a fairy?' He said, 'Start your cameras.' He came up in front of the store, looked in, put on some glasses, pushed the brim of his hat up, and went in as quite an effeminate character, started lisping something. The girl inside looked at him, and we had a lot of fun making a scene that didn't mean anything, just because Bogart was willing to take any kind of a chance. The whole relationship was that way. [Although Hawks may have forgotten, the character's feigned effeminacy was also in the book. What he and Bogart did was to elaborate on it. In the book, Marlowe comments as he enters the bookstore: 'I had my horn-rimmed sunglasses on. I put my voice high and let a bird twitter in it.'] And then that led us into another thing. We had another bookstore to go into. There was a darn good-looking girl that I'd seen the day before doing her first scene. She turned out pretty good – it was Dorothy Malone. At the end of this scene I think she said, 'Is that all you want?' He kinda looked at her and said, 'Well, I could use a drink.' She went over and took a sign on the door and turned it so it read 'Closed For The Day'. And she said, 'I just happen to have a bottle.' She was so nervous getting the drink that she was just shaking. So we stopped for lunch, and I had the property man pour a piece of lead to put in the bottom of the glass so that she could hold it. And, you know, people remember that scene. That wasn't the way it was written at all. We just did it because the girl was so damn good-looking. It taught me a great lesson, that if you make a good scene, if we could do something that was fun, the audience goes right along with you.

It seems that you were more concerned with the relationship between Bogart and Bacall than with anything else in the film.
Definitely. So was he. After we took *To Have and Have Not* out to preview it, it went over so well that Jack Warner, riding back, said,

'We'd better do another picture with those two people. Do you know a story?' I said, 'Yeah.' 'What's it like?' I said, 'Something like *Maltese Falcon*.' He said, 'Will you buy it and make it?' I never saw him again till we finished the picture and showed it to him in the projection room, and he bought my interest then and there.

Did you buy the book with your own money or with the studio's money?
I'm very pleased to say I bought that one with my own money. Made five hundred percent on it. The writers [Faulkner, Brackett, and Furthman] passed the script on to me and said, 'There are a lot of things that don't make sense.' I said, 'Good. Let's try it and see whether the audience likes that.'

When you were making the film, didn't you send a telegram to Raymond Chandler at one point asking him to explain what was happening in the story?
I asked him to explain who killed so-and-so. He wired back and said it was George somebody. I said it couldn't be George; he was down at the beach at that time. He wired back and said, 'Then I don't know either.' Actually, we didn't care. It was the first time I made a picture and just decided I wasn't going to explain things. I was just going to try and make good scenes.

It's a revolutionary thing you did, because it became the method of modern films that people don't care if the plot makes sense if it's fun. Today it's almost getting to the point of being overdone. But you were the first to really be bold enough to do that.
It's just my way of telling a story.

You made the film in 1944, and the servicemen saw it before the war was over, but the American public at home didn't see the film until 1946. And I believe that you added some scenes with Bogart and Bacall before it was released to the theatres.
Jack Warner said, 'I got such a great reaction from people, Howard. You ought to have more scenes with those two people.' I said, '*You* talk to them. If they can't behave themselves, if they have to get

54 *The Big Sleep*: Martha Vickers – 'I wanted her to be a well-dressed little girl who just happened to be a nymphomaniac.'

mushy all the time, I'm not going to stick around and make scenes with them.' They decided they could perform. I had some horses running at Santa Anita, and I said, 'I'm going to miss the races,' so I went off and wrote some scenes of Bogart and Bacall talking about a jockey who came from behind and all that kind of thing. The audience liked those scenes too.

That's one of the most outrageous examples of double-entendre *I've ever seen in a Hollywood film, talking about sex in terms of horse racing. I'm amazed you got that past the censors.*
They said they were gonna object to it, and then they thought it over and decided they liked it so much that they were gonna let it go. What they objected to was stuff that was made with the intention of being lewd, and they said I never did that, so they let me get away with murder. The end of the story was done by the censors. They read the script, and they didn't care for the end Chandler wrote. They said, 'Howard, you can't get away with this.' And I said, 'OK, you write a scene for me.' And they did, and it was a lot more violent, it was everything I wanted. I made it and was very happy about it. I said, 'I'll hire you fellows as writers.' They wrote the scene where Bogart sent a fellow out the door to get shot. That isn't exactly new, but it worked. They had vagaries about censorship. I was able to talk most of the censors out of it. In *I Was a Male War Bride*, the whole idea was Cary Grant and Ann Sheridan got married and tried for six reels to get into bed and didn't make it until they passed the Statue of Liberty coming into New York Harbor. They said, 'Howard, you can't get away with this.' And I said, 'Well, you're the boss.' They called me the next day and said, 'We got together and decided it was so much fun that you can leave it all in.'

You also got away with murder in the way you depicted the Martha Vickers character in The Big Sleep, *sucking her thumb and things like that.*
We had a great start for that little girl, where Bogart said, 'Somebody ought to housebreak her.' I made her sit around almost a day trying little things, taking a piece of hair and bringing it down

and looking at it, you know. Because I didn't want her to be Stella Stevens or somebody like that. I wanted her to be a well-dressed little girl who just happened to be a nymphomaniac.

24

Walter Brennan

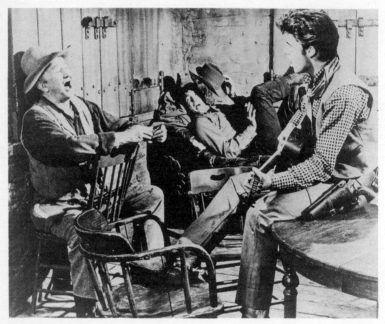

55 Walter Brennan with Dean Martin and Ricky Nelson in *Rio Bravo*.

I firmly believe that the camera likes some people and the camera dislikes other people. Somebody that the camera likes has an awful time doing wrong. Somebody that the camera dislikes has not got a chance in the world. If you look at my career, you'll find that I like actors less than I do personalities. Bogart was a great actor, but he was also a hell of a personality. Muni was a great actor but not a real personality; he interpreted things, he did them the way the writer wrote them. Eddie Robinson wasn't half as good an actor as he was supposed to be, but he was a hell of a personality, and he could be egged into doing things. But I think Walter Brennan was the greatest example of a personality that I've ever used. Once you look at him you start to laugh. When I was casting *Barbary Coast*, a very smart production man said, 'You know that character you were talking about the other day? I know somebody exactly like that.' I said, 'Well, why don't I see him?' 'This fellow hasn't done anything. I don't think he's ever spoken a line. He's just an extra man, but, my God, he's just what you described. I don't know whether he can act or anything.' And I said, 'Bring him in, but put him into costume, give him some lines. It'll save some time. I won't have to see him two or three times.' So he brought in Walter Brennan, and I looked at him and laughed. I said, 'Mr Brennan, did they give you some lines?' He said, 'Yeah.' I said, 'Do you know them?' 'Uh-huh.' 'Do you want to read them?' And he said, 'With or without?' I said, 'With or without what?' He said, 'Teeth.' He was in then. He didn't have to read the lines. I laughed again and said, 'Without.' He turned around, took his teeth out, turned back around, and started talking to me. He was supposed to work three days, and I kept him a month doing 'Old Atrocity'. The next picture I put him in [*Come and Get It*], the writer described him as 'the strongest man in the North woods'. Here was this little Brennan. He got an Academy Award for playing in that. He worked in five pictures for me, and he had parts in only two of the pictures. The rest of the time I'd just call him up. He didn't worry about it – he'd do anything you wanted him to do. I'd say, 'Walter, I've got a picture.' 'Fine,' he said, 'I'll be over tomorrow.' And he'd come over, and he'd say, 'Where's the contract?' I'd say, 'I haven't got a contract yet.' 'Oh, I want to sign a contract.' I said, 'OK,' and the next day he came in, signed the contract, and said, 'Now tell me the story.' And I said, 'Now, you so-and-so, I don't have to tell you the story. I've got a contract with you.' He read the story, and he came in and said, 'Gee, that's a great story. What part do I play?' 'Oh,' I said, 'there's one line in the script, it says, "The cook's name is Groot." That's the part you're gonna play.' He said, 'What do we do?' I said, 'Remember how we met, that "with or without teeth"? Well, at the beginning of the cattle drive, you're gonna lose your teeth in a poker game with an Indian. Then every time you want to eat, you're gonna

133

have to get 'em back from the Indian.' 'Oh,' he said, 'we can't do that.' That was *Red River*. We just made up every scene that he was in. But those kind of people are very few and far between. There are some people who have a quality of going in where you need somebody. No matter what your story is, they make it better, and I try to use those people. In *Twentieth Century*, the little fellow [Etienne Girardot] ran around the train pasting slogans on the backs of the characters. He became a very, very important person, and that's how I came to believe in a character like that. I try to do as much of it as I can. I hate faceless people who speak words and you don't know what the devil they're doing or why. I like 'em to have more or less of a motive. When I was in trouble, I called on Brennan. He always came through. On *To Have and Have Not*, Bogey had a hangover one day, and he wasn't too bright. 'God,' I said, 'you're great to work with a hangover. You can't do a goddam thing, can you?' He said, 'I guess not.' I said, 'Walter, come on over here. You stand in between Bogey and this other fella. And when Bogey starts talking about numbers, you start counting on your hand, and you shake your head. Do anything you feel like doing. For Chrissake, make this scene better.' You laughed all the way through the scene, at him doing it in *To Have and Have Not*. When I couldn't get Brennan I got somebody else, but he's damn hard to replace. I would have liked Brennan playing the part of the old fellow in *El Dorado*, but I couldn't get him, so I used Arthur Hunnicutt. I thought Hunnicutt was good. But Brennan had an amazing quality, to be able to play anything and do it right.

What's the function of the old man character played by Brennan or Hunnicutt in your westerns?
I think it's a way of telling the story, telling the plot. They tell it in an interesting way. You're not conscious that you're getting the plot; you're being amused by him. I don't want to use a half-wit, and I don't like psychiatric characters. I like people that they like. When I was doing *Rio Bravo* with Brennan, he amazed me with the first scene he did. I said, 'What the hell is going on here? Are you going to play that goddam television show that you've been doing, for me? Do you think I'm gonna make a *Real McCoy* out of it? This is

supposed to be a crabby, evil, nasty old man.' 'Oh, God,' he said. I said to Wayne, 'Come on, Duke, let's go over and play a game of checkers and let this dumbbell think up what he's got to do.' So for fifteen minutes we stayed away, and he just sat there. Then he came in and he was really a bastard. It was easy the rest of the time.

25

John Ford

What do you think you have in common with John Ford?
Well, a great deal. He was a good director when I started, and I copied him every time I could. It's just as if you were a writer, you would read Hemingway and Faulkner and John Dos Passos and Willa Cather and a lot of people like that. We were very good friends. I don't think I've done nearly as good as Ford has on some things. I think he's got the greatest vision for a tableau, a long-shot, of any man. One of my favourite pictures of all time is *The Quiet Man*, which I think was just a beautiful picture. Ford, oh, he's done some things that are just fabulous. And he was the first man to do them. Every time I run into a scene that I think Ford does very well, I stop things and think, 'What would he have done there?' And then I go ahead and do it, because he gets more use out of a bad sky – he goes right on shooting whether the weather's bad or good, and he gets fabulous effects. I was making a picture with Wayne, *Red River*. We had a burial scene. And the cameraman [Russell Harlan] said, 'We better hurry, there's a cloud coming across that mountain right behind.' So I said to Wayne, 'Now, look, you go out there – if you forget your lines, just say anything, keep talking until I tell you to come on in. We'll make the sound afterwards.' And I waited until the cloud got near, thought of Ford, and started the scene. Then we started the burial service, and the cloud passed right over the whole scene. I told Jack, I said, 'Hey, I've made one almost as good as you can do – you better go and see it.'

Is there anything you think you can do better than Ford?
Oh, I think I couldn't do his brand of humour. His brand of humour was kind of a bucolic travesty of an Irishman, kind of overdrawn characters. I certainly know that I made better comedies than he did.

But I don't think I made better westerns. I don't think *Red River* is better than his westerns. He's a great storyteller. We always used to talk about the differences between the way we did scenes. He'd tell me what things he stole from me, and I'd tell him what things I stole from him, but we did them so differently that it didn't make any difference whether we stole them. He said if he had a scene that he didn't think was good enough, he'd do it in a long shot rather than try to punch it up. If I've got a scene like that I just try to do it as quick as I can. I don't think we worked very much the same. I told him he was corny. He said, 'Well, you're so damned sarcastic.' Jack was quite a guy. I saw more of him than anybody, almost, in his last few months because I'd just drop over to the house. He spent most of his time looking at old, old westerns on television – you know, those cheap westerns that were made in about a week. And he was still bright; he kept his senses. The last time I went out to see him, he said goodbye to me. I walked out and stopped to speak to his daughter, and he yelled, 'Is Howard gone yet?' She said no. 'I want to see him!' He said, 'I want to say goodbye to you.' I said goodbye. He yelled again, 'Is he still there?' And he said, 'I want to say *goodbye* to you.' So I called Duke Wayne and said, 'Duke, you'd better get down here. I think he's going to die.' Duke got a helicopter and came down here, and the next day he died. Peter Bogdanovich did a damn good story about that [in *New York* magazine]. He got it a little bit messed up, but it made a good ending for his story.

26

The Western

There are not very many stories that you can do about the West that are any good. You haven't got an awful lot of choice. The western is the simplest form of drama – a gun, death – and they all fall, really, into two kinds. One is the history of the beginning of the West, the story of the pioneers, which was the story of *Red River*. Then there's the phase when law and order comes. You've got a sheriff – sometimes you had a bad sheriff; sometimes you had a good one. There are only a few forms. But every time a first-rate director makes a western, he usually ends up with a pretty-good picture, because a western's good entertainment, it's dramatic. Ford made great westerns. He was the best director of the bunch. Stevens made a damn good western, *Shane*. I haven't made a lot. People say I've made a lot of 'em, but I've made five westerns, and I've made forty pictures altogether. If you call *Hatari!* a western, which I do in my way of thinking about it, why, I've made six of 'em. Westerns just happen to be something that I like. I like to get out of the studio, I like to get out in the air, and I think they've been fun to do. I've read and studied a lot on it. I spent two or three years in Europe in the 1950s, came back, and they said, 'What do you want to do?' I said, 'A western.' 'Oh, you don't want to do a western. Nobody's made one for a long time.' I said, 'Yeah, I do.' So they said 'OK,' and I made *Rio Bravo*. It was very popular, started westerns all over again. Then when all this bunch of new stories came in, with sick people and psychopaths and nudity and everything like that, I didn't know where the devil it was gonna go. Things are changing so rapidly now. I talked to an exhibitor the other day, and he said booking a picture today is like playing Russian roulette. I agree with him. And I said to Wayne, 'Do you want to make a couple of westerns?' He said, 'Damn right.' And we made 'em.

56 *The Big Sky*: Two men and a girl – Elizabeth Coyotte Threatt, Kirk Douglas and Dewey Martin.

57 *The Big Sky*: Hawks with Douglas.

Westerns have been in eclipse again in the 1970s. Do you think they'll make another comeback?

They're not going to come back till they get somebody who can make 'em. Not these eastern fellows who don't know one end of a horse from another. Some people have tried silly things, like a picture called *The Left-Handed Gun*, which compared a western gunman with a modern-day hophead or something. It's no good; it doesn't live up to what people want in a western. There are good western stories, but they don't get the right people to play 'em. They don't get the right people to write 'em.

What do you think of The Wild Bunch?

I thought it was pretty bad. Somebody asked me about it, and I said, 'Well, he doesn't know how to direct. I can kill four men, take 'em to the morgue, and bury 'em before he gets one down to the ground in slow motion.' All I saw was a lot of red paint and blood running. I don't think a good director has to utilize that stuff.

Have you seen the Italian westerns?

There were two or three of them with Eastwood, and a couple of them went very well, and now they've fallen off pretty bad. They're not very well made now. They're not well made at all. I can't sit through them.

What do you think of Wayne's picture The Cowboys?

Awful. I don't like children too much in pictures. I like 'em in real life, but in pictures they're corny. I liked *Butch Cassidy*. It was a damn well-written story. And I liked the Indian picture, *Tell Them Willie Boy Is Here*.

Most of the recent westerns have tried to debunk the mythology of the West. What do you think about that?

You mean there are people around today who remember what it was like?

27

John Wayne

58 'Wayne helped Angie Dickinson so much in *Rio Bravo*.'

John Wayne represents more force, more power, than anybody else on the screen. And I think both Ford and I succeeded in making pretty good scenes with him. When Ford was dying, we used to discuss how tough it was to make a good western without Wayne. Now, that's just our two viewpoints about it, but maybe you can tell me somebody who's made westerns as good as Wayne has. Cary Grant and I have been talking about him doing a western playing a consumptive dentist. He'd like very much to play it. We've already mapped out the best scenes. But he wouldn't be quite the same as if Wayne did it. If Duke heard I was going to do a western without him, he'd call up and say, 'Can't you write me in?'

You were talking before about personalities and actors – is Wayne as much of an actor as he is a personality?
Well, John Wayne is pretty goddam good, or he wouldn't have been leading things for so long. They don't think of him as being an actor, but Christ, he's a damn good actor. He does everything, and he makes you believe it. He's just a different form of an actor. A Broadway actor would be inclined to look down his nose at him, but by the very number of pictures he's made and the fact that people still like him, I'd say Wayne has to be pretty real.

His professionalism really shines through when you see him with a young performer who isn't very smooth, such as a couple of the actors in Rio Lobo. *Jennifer O'Neill couldn't begin to hold the screen with Wayne.*
Oh, she was a damn fool. But Wayne helped Angie Dickinson so much in *Rio Bravo*. He helped Charlene Holt in *El Dorado*. You start with the idea that if you don't get a damn good actor with Wayne, he's going to blow him right off the screen, not just by the fact that he's good, but by his power, his strength.

What if you've got a man or a woman who you know is not going to be able to handle Wayne on the screen?
Then you're out of luck. There wasn't much I could do in the picture you're talking about. The two boys in there just couldn't handle Wayne. And the girl was no good, so we were out of luck. Most of

the leading men today, the younger men especially, are a little bit effeminate. There's no toughness. McQueen and Eastwood don't compare with Wayne.

Wayne has a reputation for being a very tough guy with directors.
He *is* tough. The only people who could handle him were Ford and myself.

Why is that?
Ford put Wayne in *Stagecoach*. I put him in *Red River*. Wayne did a hell of a job in *Red River*, and Jack Ford said, 'I never knew the big son of a bitch could act.' So every time I made a picture with Wayne, Ford would come around and watch.

And as a matter of fact, after Red River, *Ford began putting Wayne into more complex parts in his own films. He made* She Wore a Yellow Ribbon, *where he played an old man, and he was brilliant. But* Red River *was the first time he played somebody older than his years.*
Yes. In *Red River*, he wasn't sure whether he wanted to play an old man, and I said, 'Duke, you're going to be one pretty soon, why don't you get some practice?' He said, 'How the hell am I gonna play one?' 'Well,' I said, 'watch me getting up. That's the way to play it.' Ford said he didn't know Wayne could act, but I said he could do anything if you've got enough guts to tell him what to do.

Do you think Ford condescended to Wayne?
He treated him a little like a beginner.

He treated him quite terribly, from what I've heard.
Oh, yes. But Wayne adored him.

Ford was the only man who could abuse Wayne for forty-five years and get away with it. But you treated him like an equal. Watching the Plimpton documentary on the making of Rio Lobo, *I felt that you and Wayne kidded each other, but it was a real give-and-take. Neither one had the upper hand. You respected each other.*

Well, Wayne never read a script that I had. He'd always want me to tell him. 'What am I supposed to do in this?' 'Well, you're supposed to give the impression of this and this.' And he'd say, 'OK.' When I'd start to tell him one of my stories, he'd always say, 'I don't want to hear it. I've never liked your stories and they always turn out good.' He'd never learn lines before I talked to him, because he said that threw him off. He could memorize two pages of lines in three or four minutes. He never squawks about anything. He's the easiest person that I've ever worked with. Because he never says anything about it, he just goes ahead and does it.

He has the reputation when he works with the younger directors that he sort of directs himself. He gets active in the direction of the scenes. Did you ever have any trouble with him like that?
I told him one time, 'I hear you're pretty tough about that.' 'Oh,' he said, 'you and Ford spoil me, you know.' That was all there was to it. He wanted to kind of direct himself, but I wouldn't say that there was one moment when he was – sometimes he'll go around shaking his head or something like that, and so I say, 'What the hell's the matter with you?' 'Something's wrong!' And he can't tell you where it is or what is wrong, but he'll say, 'Now, wait a minute. We'll try a rehearsal again, and I'll just do this [gestures] when they come to the wrong part.' Then I find out what's wrong and write a few lines and say, 'Try this.' And he beams all over and says, 'That works good.' What he meant was he felt wrong. And he was right. He has the instinct of how to make a good scene.

What is your opinion of the direction of The Alamo *and* The Green Berets?
Pretty bad. I think Duke is a much better actor than he is a director.

Do you plan to make another picture with him?
I don't want Wayne any more unless I get a story that's right for him. Duke called me a while ago and said, 'Howard, let's make a picture. Everything I've been doing has been lousy.' I said, 'Well, I haven't found a story.' He said, 'I found one. I'd play the part of an old gunfighter. He's walking down the street, and some guy calls him

out, but he's lost his glasses, and the man is hazy. Finally a girl comes running up and brings him some glasses, and he shoots the guy.' I said, 'Duke, all your life you've stood for something. Why should you throw it away for something like this?' He said, 'Don't you think it's funny?' I said, 'No, I think it's pitiful.' 'What about *True Grit*?' he said. I said, '*True Grit* was an exaggerated thing, and it got by because the director [Henry Hathaway] didn't know whether he was making a comedy or a drama.' Right now, when you pay Wayne a million dollars, I wouldn't say he was worth it unless you had the right story. And another thing, I'll tell you very frankly, I'm not very interested in making pictures about old men. Like in *Rio Lobo* – Wayne had a hard time getting on and off his horse; he can't move like a big cat the way he used to. He has to hold his belly in; he's a different kind of person.

I thought in El Dorado *especially you made use of Wayne's age in a very moving way, showing how he was slowing up.*
Oh, we made use of it, yeah. But you can't do a love story with him now, and he doesn't want love stories. Well, it makes it pretty hard to find a story. I could have made a good picture out of the ransom picture he did. *Big Jake*, was that the one? I could have done a good job on that.

Wayne and Katharine Hepburn recently made a western together, Rooster Cogburn. *It wasn't very good, but they were interesting together. Would you like to work with the two of them at this point?*
I would love to make a picture with the two of them. They're both great to work with, if you find a story that really fits them. I told Wayne one about a month ago. He said, 'Dammit, you're gonna make me old long before I get old.' And I said, 'OK, don't do it. I'll just hang on to it for a while.'

What story was that?
I would like to try a story I made called *Come and Get It*; they put a different ending on it that messed it up. I think you could turn that into a western. It is the story of two friends, two older friends, and

they met a girl, who was beautifully played in *Come and Get It* by Frances Farmer. One guy was in love with her but he wanted money, he wanted position and everything, so he married a rich girl and left her. And his friend married the girl that he'd left, knowing that the girl was in love with the other man. And they had a daughter, and the other man fell in love with the daughter. He was really repeating his love affair with the girl. It's still a good story.

Would Wayne play the Edward Arnold part?
Yeah.

But how about the scenes where he's supposed to be a younger man? How could you do that?
Oh, with a lot of gauze – I don't know, that's why I'm hesitating. I think I would rather age somebody, like in *Red River*. I'd rather take Clint Eastwood and make him age. Wayne's getting to be fat and heavy.

Actually, Red River *almost is* Come and Get It *as a western. It's the story of an older man and a younger man who are like father and foster son, and they battle each other and wind up loving the same woman, who is a surrogate for the woman the older man left.*
Yes, I never thought of that.

28

Red River

I brought along a magazine, Film Comment, *because I want to show you something Borden Chase [co-writer of* Red River *and author of the original story] said about you. They never gave you a chance to reply, so I thought in all fairness you should be given a chance to go on the record with a response. [Hawks spent about five minutes reading Chase's remarks on* Red River *from an interview with Jim Kitses in the 'Hollywood Screenwriter' issue of* Film Comment, *Winter 1970–71. Briefly, Chase attacked Hawks for changing parts of his script, for historical inaccuracies, and for shortening John Ireland's part because Ireland was 'fooling around with Howard's girl'. Hawks chuckled occasionally as he read the interview.]*

He must have been drinking when he said this, because he's so full of shit. That's funny. Borden Chase is the kind of a writer that imagines an awful lot of things; he does quite a bit of drinking. I bought the story from him and asked him to work on it. I'd been working on a story of the King Ranch. The fellow that asked me to make it owned the King Ranch; we were friends. I thought it was a good story. I chased down a Catholic priest down there, and the priest told me many, many things about the King Ranch. I talked to the fellow that owned the ranch, and I said, 'I'm not going to do a milk-and-water version,' so I gave it up, but I had a lot of stuff left over. And every time I tried to change Borden Chase's story he objected to it. He did not work on it at the same time [Charles] Schnee did and all that stuff he talked about. I got Schnee, and we rewrote the story. We rewrote a whole bunch of things. He hadn't finished the story for the simple reason that when he finished it, *The Saturday Evening Post* didn't like it. They said they'd take it if he'd rewrite it. I thought the way he wrote it was pretty lousy. I never introduced Schnee as my secretary or any of that crap. He just got angry at the idea that we

59 *Red River*: Hawks with Wayne and Joanne Dru.

were going to change the story that he wrote. We were going to make a movie, not write a serial for *The Saturday Evening Post.* Where he says he was telling Wayne how to make that walk through the cattle – he didn't even know that was going to be done. He never saw that until it was done; it was not in the script. You don't have to tell Wayne anything about walking through cattle; Wayne knew. He took his horse right to the cattle, and then he walked through 'em. They just accidentally got in his way, and he just shoved 'em and kept on walking. Then Chase goes on, 'Duke said, "We're dropping Cherry Valance." I said, "What do you mean?" "Well," he said, "he's fooling around with Howard's girl." I can't remember her name, she's married now.' Actually what happened was that I got tired of this actor [John Ireland] getting drunk every night, losing his gun and his hat, smoking marijuana, and I just cut the hell out of his scenes and gave them to somebody else. We just couldn't take time from work for this man; one of the worst things for morale when you're making a picture is to stand a guy up in front of the camera. And he wasn't fooling around with my girl; he was fooling around with the girl who was playing in the picture [Joanne Dru]. I'd never been out to dinner with her or anything else. So that's why we cut out his part. He sends me these wires saying, 'You gave me one chance, please give me another, I won't blow it.' Chase says he was a big guy with horses. Well, I raised horses for fifteen years. I knew them goddam well. And he said, 'The phony parts of the picture, number one, are the guns. Everybody was carrying a six-shooter around. Well, there weren't six of them in all of Texas, and they were owned by the Rangers.' I got a bunch of letters about using six-shooters, but I didn't want to stop a scene to have a guy reload his gun before he could fire. He says, 'He talks about being a western director. You know what that fool did? He had five thousand head out in the grass, they ate it all off, and they had to hand-feed them. They had to hand-feed five thousand head, and they were white-face because you can't get that many longhorn.' You *can't* get that many longhorn, so we put the longhorn up front. But anyway, we bought Mexican cattle, hand-fed them, and made a hell of a lot of money selling them after the picture was over. Borden Chase wasn't content with writing a story; he wanted to tell you how to do it. I wouldn't say that he was the greatest judge of how to do it. He never had another good picture. Look, I liked his story, but I didn't care much for Chase. I thought he was a goddam idiot. When he came down here to work, he brought a peroxide blonde with him, and he was a lot more interested in getting back in the box with her than he was in working on the story. I never had any luck in getting the writer of a thing to do the scenario except Bill Faulkner.

I understand that Red River *went way over budget and way over schedule. When that happened, were you under pressure to complete the film and bring it back?*
Did the man who made out the budget tell you that? Because the budget was made out, and there was no allowance for travelling. We had to transport fifteen hundred head of cattle all around Arizona, and we had to transport ourselves, too, so we went about $800,000 over making the picture. But they decided they'd made a mistake. They'd forgotten to put that in the budget.

I read in a history of United Artists that you tried to withhold Red River *from distribution for about a year as part of a move against UA by several producers. Could you explain what was behind that?*
I thought they were a bunch of cheats. Later on I found that out. I ran into a man who said, 'I want to thank you so much,' and I said, 'Why?' He said, 'I made a fortune out of that picture.' I said, 'What did you pay for it?' He said, '$50,000, and I gave the United Artists salesman $50,000 too.' So then I knew they were cheating. They do that, and you have to be very careful about those things. It probably takes as long to watch them as it does to make the movie.

How sympathetic did you intend John Wayne to be in the film? Quite often the script almost makes him come off as a heavy.
I wasn't worried a bit about him being sympathetic. See, I don't read the script. I just go out and make scenes. I hadn't any idea of making Wayne a heavy. I thought he had a good part that resembled very much the story of the King Ranch, a man who got in on the beginning of things and built one of the greatest ranches in the world. And that's what I was trying to do with Wayne.

60 *Red River*: Wayne and Clift – 'Hell, with the characters that I had and
their relationship, that was the only ending you could possibly use.'

Why doesn't Montgomery Clift shoot Wayne at the end?
I still don't believe in killing people and making a picture end with
death, but I did it in *Only Angels Have Wings* very successfully.
People have talked about the ending of *Red River* – hell, with the
characters that I had and their relationship, that was the only ending
you could possibly use. Anybody who says it different isn't a student
of characters. Because Wayne had a distinct character, and Monty
Clift had a distinct character, and the only way they could end up
was just the way they did. If they couldn't understand that
relationship, why then, they . . .

*How did you come to use Clift? It was his first film. Was he an
unusual choice for a western at that time?*
I didn't think he was unusual when I chose him. I wanted a young
man. I had another cowboy who won five straight rodeos. I thought
I better try him out first, and so he rode into a scene and fell off and
broke his arm. I made a test of Clift, and I thought he was good.

Wayne took a look at him and said, 'Howard, this is not going to work.' I said, 'Why?' He said, 'That kid isn't going to stand up to me.' I said, 'Well, why don't we make the first scene?' It was a scene alongside a wagon, and Wayne was talking tough; Clift had a coffee cup, and he had it up to his face all the time. He never changed expression or anything. And after the scene Duke said, 'I watched that kid all the time. There's only one thing that still bothers me, whether he can keep up with me in a fight. We're supposed to have a fight.' I said, 'Duke, I don't think *I* can keep up with you in a fight, but if I got a lucky chance and kicked you in the jaw, I think I'd have a good chance.' 'OK,' he said. And we had Monty kick him in the jaw. We took four days, and my arm's still sore from trying to show Montgomery Clift how to throw a punch, every move. I think we made a respectable fight. As for his western ability, he went out every morning about 6:30 with one of the best cowboys that I knew, and he came back in time to get a late supper. In a month he could really handle a horse, and he really could do anything with a gun. I thought he was a perfect choice for the thing. He's by far better than any other person we tested. So I can't really answer why did I choose him except I thought he was good.

29

Marilyn Monroe

61 Marilyn Monroe with Cary Grant in *Monkey Business*.

Marilyn Monroe was the most frightened little girl who had no confidence in her ability. She was afraid to come on the screen. Very strange girl. And yet she had this strange effect when she was photographed. Nobody dated her, nobody took her out, nobody paid any attention to her. She'd sit on the set with practically nothing on, and a pretty extra girl would walk by and everybody'd whistle. But she got out in front of the camera, and the camera liked her, and all of a sudden she was a great sex symbol. Fortunately, I had her in a couple of the first pictures that she did [*Monkey Business* and *Gentlemen Prefer Blondes*], when she wasn't worried. And also I had Jane Russell's help in making *Gentlemen Prefer Blondes*. We had a lot of fun doing the picture, but there were a lot of times when I was ready to give up the ghost. Jane Russell would say, 'Look at me – all he wants you to do is such-and-such a thing.' And Marilyn would say to her, 'Why didn't you tell me?' But I had an easy time compared to some of the directors who worked with her afterward. Because after she got very important she became more and more frightened, and she just didn't want to come out and do a scene. She didn't think she was good enough to do the things that she did.

She was always better in fantastic material, wasn't she? Like in Gentlemen Prefer Blondes?
There wasn't a real thing about her. Everything was completely unreal. They tried to make her play real parts in a couple of pictures, and the pictures were disasters. *Gentlemen Prefer Blondes* was the first one where she really went good, and then they had no sense to stick with that.

62 Marilyn Monroe singing 'Diamonds Are a Girl's Best Friend' in *Gentlemen Prefer Blondes.*

63 Music: *Gentlemen Prefer Blondes* – Marilyn Monroe and Jane Russell.

We went through a phase of putting lousy music into pictures where inferior musicians copied great masters. It just became ridiculous, with about twenty violins and fifteen cellos and woodwinds and all of that stuff. I worked with [Dimitri] Tiomkin, whom I thought was a pretty good musician, but when we made *Hatari!*, I said to Dimi, 'Look, I don't want one violin. I don't want one cello. I don't want any woodwind. I want native instruments or something else that you can think of.' He said, 'That's a great idea, boss.' Then he called me the next day and said, 'You were fooling, weren't you?' And I said, 'You're fired, Dimi.' He said, 'What do you mean?' I said, 'Anybody who doesn't want to do what I tell them to do, I don't want.' Henry Mancini was doing some little television show [*Peter Gunn*], and I thought, 'Gee, this guy is good.' I got him in and said, 'I'd like to have you do this picture, but no violins, no cellos –' I went through the whole routine with him. He said, 'OK.' I said, 'You use a violin, and I'll fire you.' He came to me one day, and he said, 'I guess I'm going to get fired.' I said, 'Why?' and he said, 'Come on down on the set.' He had a violin being played with a calliope. They were doing 'Baby Elephant Walk'. I said, 'OK, you're not fired.' The only score up until then that I liked was *The Third Man*, where they just had a zither. I thought that was just fine, because I got so sick and tired of this music. Tiomkin was pretty good. Tiomkin didn't steal as much as the others. When he got up to get an Academy Award, he thanked all the famous composers.

You like to use song scenes, such as in Rio Bravo, *where you took a lot of heat for using Ricky Nelson because he was a pop star of the time. But actually, if you look at the film today, he's quite charming, and the scene of him singing with Dean Martin and Walter Brennan is one of the highlights of the picture. Can you explain at what point you believe it's germane to insert a song?*
Well, when *Rio Bravo* was released in Japan, they had a great big picture of Ricky Nelson and a little picture of John Wayne on the other side. And we got a million dollars more than we usually did without that, so I thought that worked out pretty well.

64 Music: *Only Angels Have Wings* – Jean Arthur.

65 Music: *To Have and Have Not* – Lauren Bacall with Hoagy
Carmichael at piano.

I saw the film when I was twelve years old, and the only reason I went to see it was because Ricky Nelson was in it. At that time I didn't know who you were. So it helped the box office here too.

I didn't know you appreciated music so much. You know, when you've got some talent, your job is to use it. Because you're making pictures of the personality.

I understand you shot a scene for El Dorado *of Robert Mitchum singing. Why didn't you use it?*

Mitchum's a pretty good singer. But my son said, 'Dad, a sheriff shouldn't sing.' So I cut it out.

In Ball of Fire, *you have Stanwyck singing 'Drum Boogie' in the nightclub with Krupa playing the drums, then you do a variant on the song as 'Match Boogie', Krupa doing it with a pair of matches on a matchbox. Why did you add that second part to it?*

That was made up just for fun. I think I saw Krupa doing it with a matchbox, and it looked so good I said, 'Hey, we'll put it in.' So we made up a scene. Took about two hours to do it.

There's one of your rare sentimental moments in that film, when the professors sing 'Genevieve'.

When you're doing a story about old people you can afford to be sentimental, you know. God, I was responsible for starting 'Jeannie with the Light-Brown Hair' up again [the theme music from *Barbary Coast*]. I've regretted that ever since.

You seem fond of jazz. You use it in Ball of Fire *and also in* A Song Is Born.

I happen to like jazz very much. I know a lot of – or did know a lot of – good jazz players. We had a session at the house once with Benny Goodman and I think Mel Powell, one of the great piano players; Hoagy Carmichael; and, oddly enough, Piatigorsky and Kreisler. And I remember Piatigorsky looking at Kreisler and saying, 'Play, Fishface, play!' I've got a lot of records somewhere made by all that bunch. So it's fun to get out there and make that kind of stuff. You have to make it right on the set; you can't write it beforehand. You just have to go out and do it. I only use playback when I have to.

What about multiple cameras on musical numbers? Did you ever do that?
I did a musical called *Gentlemen Prefer Blondes*, and I didn't do the production numbers. I didn't have any desire to. I did the little numbers that were part of the story. As a matter of fact, I had an agreement that I didn't have to use the Fox music department to do it. We did a quiet little song that Marilyn sang, and stuff that Jane Russell and Marilyn did that are scenes with music in them; they didn't need a lot of choreography or anything like that.

Is it true that Lauren Bacall's singing voice in To Have and Have Not *was dubbed by Andy Williams?*
We had a hell of a time trying to find a girl to sing with as low a voice as Bacall's. So I got Andy Williams, and we took all the music he recorded and let Bacall mouth it to his singing. But she was singing at the same time, and I thought she sounded better than Andy Williams. So we went back and did the whole thing over again. It was all her singing. There was another picture where she sang, *The Big Sleep*. And that was her voice too.

31

Themes and Variations: Three Westerns

Rio Bravo was made because I didn't like a picture called *High Noon*. I saw *High Noon* at about the same time I saw another western picture, and we were talking about western pictures, and they asked me if I liked it, and I said, 'Not particularly.' I didn't think a good sheriff was going to go running around town like a chicken with his head off asking for help, and finally his Quaker wife had to save him. That isn't my idea of a good western sheriff. I said that a good sheriff would turn around and say, 'How good are you? Are you good enough to take the best man they've got?' The fellow would probably say no, and he'd say, 'Well, then I'd just have to take care of you.' And that scene was in *Rio Bravo*. Then I said I saw another picture where the sheriff caught a prisoner, and the prisoner taunted him and made him perspire and worry and everything by saying, 'Wait till my friends catch up with you.' And I said, 'That's a lot of nonsense, the sheriff would say, "You better hope your friends *don't* catch up with you, 'cause you'll be the first man to die."' While we were doing all this, they said, 'Why don't you make a picture the other way?' And I said, 'OK,' and we made *Rio Bravo* the exact opposite from *High Noon* and this other picture, I think it was called *3:10 to Yuma*.

The credits of Rio Bravo *say the script by Jules Furthman and Leigh Brackett is based on a story by B. H. McCampbell. Who is that?*
My daughter [Barbara Hawks McCampbell]. She was trying to write, and she had an idea that she thought would be good, so I paid her for the story. She had the idea that some outlaws were holed up, and to get 'em out they threw dynamite and shot the dynamite. We used that in the end of the story. So out of the things that I didn't like in other westerns, plus the stuff that Barbie had, we made a pretty good story out of it.

There are several things in Rio Bravo *that are similar to* Under-world, *which you and Furthman also helped write.*
I stole two things, the dollar in the spittoon and the girl's name, Feathers.

Also, in Underworld *George Bancroft is helping his best friend, Clive Brook, who is a drunk, just like John Wayne and Dean Martin in* Rio Bravo. *And when somebody offers Bancroft help, he turns it down by saying, 'People don't help me – I help people,' which is something Wayne could have said in* Rio Bravo.
Yeah, well, you know, I always liked that story.

You remade Rio Bravo *twice, as* El Dorado *and* Rio Lobo.
They weren't remakes. Did you ever read Hemingway? Did you ever find any similarities between stories? Hemingway always stole from himself. He always wrote a certain kind of a thing that he was good at. If we make a picture that's a top-biller, that the people like, we're inclined to want to do a different version of the same picture. And if a director has a story that he likes and he tells it, very often he looks at the picture and says, 'I could do that better if I did it again,' so I'd do it again. I'll keep on doing them, in a different way. I'm not a damn bit interested in whether somebody thinks this is a copy of it, because the copy made more money than the original, and I was very pleased with it. We found that they liked *Rio Bravo*, and oddly enough, I think they liked *El Dorado* better. Although I think that *Rio Bravo* was a better picture. It's a lot of fun to see what you can do that's a little different when you do one and you do the other. When we came to a certain place in *Rio Bravo*, we had our choice between going in this direction and going in that direction. But we made notes to remember, because we said, 'This is so good we can use it sometime.' We ended up with enough good notes to make another movie, so we made another movie. When we started on *El Dorado*, I said to the writer [Brackett], the same one who worked on *Rio Bravo*, 'Now, look, we had a very good boy gunman in *Rio Bravo*; let's make a boy who can't shoot at all.' That wasn't the same, was it? In *Rio Bravo*, Wayne was the sheriff, and his deputy was a drunk. In *El Dorado*, Bob Mitchum was the sheriff, and *he*

66 *El Dorado*: James Caan.

67 *El Dorado*: Howard Hawks and Robert Mitchum – 'I think he's one of the best actors I know.'

was the drunk, and the deputy was perfectly sober. We changed it from Wayne being a sheriff to Wayne being a gunman. You had Dean Martin as the drunk in one, Mitchum in the other. They're two different people. There are always two ways to go, you can go any which way, and we knew that both ways were good. We just turned the whole thing around. We did everything by opposites. I don't think there's anything you can do except opposites. I don't think there's any connection between the two stories. I've heard people say so, but I don't think they've *seen* both of them. There *is* a similarity, but it comes from style, it comes from writing, it comes from the fact that it's made in the same part of the country, because the costumes are very much the same. We found people liked it, and so we didn't mind it a bit. Now, *Rio Lobo* is quite different because it starts in the war between the North and the South, so you don't quite think it's going to be a western; then it changes to the western. You can probably say that western is a lot like the other two. Sure. You've got fellows with guns, and one of them's a sheriff . . . you know, there isn't much you can do. The last picture we made [*Rio Lobo*], I called up Wayne and said, 'Duke, I've got a story.' He said, 'I can't make it for a year. I'm all tied up.' And I said, 'Well, that's all right, it'll take me a year to get it finished.' He said, 'Good, I'll be all ready.' And he came down on location, and he said, 'What's this about?' And I told him the story. He never even read it. He didn't know anything about it.

Didn't it sound familiar to him, though?
Yes, he said, 'Do I get to play the drunk this time?'

What was the scene you actually shot for Rio Bravo *but cut out and used in* El Dorado*?*
It was the idea of a bunch of horsemen coming around a corner and one man throws himself on the ground. He says, 'A man can't shoot you because a horse won't step on a man.' Now, that is not strictly true, a horse will step on a man, but he'll *try* not to. We killed off so many of the bad men that I said, 'Well, this is getting to be funny – let's cut this sequence out.' It was one of the best sequences we had. They said, 'You're gonna cut that out?' And I said, 'Yeah, but I'm

going to do it in the next picture,' and I did, and it worked out beautifully. I even thought about trying to use the same film because it was the same street. I took it out for a very good reason. It was too much of a good thing. If you get too much violence you lose the whole thing.

One reason I admire Rio Bravo *so much is that it sticks so close to one strong plot line.*
What did the story take, three days?

Yes. In El Dorado *you meander around a bit more. It's more relaxed, isn't it? There's more room for side incidents.*
Yeah, but you see, you hook things together. You don't really say what it is, but Wayne shoots a kid in the stomach, so he wants to help that family. He feels that he wronged 'em. So that gives him a reason. He joins with his old friend because his friend turned into a drunk because Wayne took a girl away from him. Pretty good plot in *El Dorado*, even though it wanders around, it isn't as condensed. I couldn't do *Rio Bravo* again, you know what I mean? We had to hunt up something new. You can let a thing wander around. *Big Sleep* wandered around a little bit, but almost every scene in *Big Sleep* was a pretty good scene to look at.

I thought James Caan was very funny as the inept gunman in El Dorado, *because usually the men in your pictures are very professional. It was funny the way John Wayne immediately gave up on him, didn't try to show him how to do it or anything, just gave up instantly.*
Well, I think a professional would, after he saw Jimmy Caan shoot.

Caan had a sense of humour and a loose quality that he doesn't often have in other films. How did you get that?
It was Caan's first good part, and he accepted anything I'd tell him without any argument. He's a damn good actor, and we started rolling the more we got into it. He got a lot of laughs playing it perfectly serious. He didn't know he was playing a comedy. Not until he went to see the preview. He came up to me and said, 'Why

68 *El Dorado*: Michele Carey with Mitchum and Wayne.

didn't you tell me I was playing a comic part?' And I said, 'You'd have spoiled it. You'd have tried to be funny.'

Mitchum is extraordinarily good in El Dorado, *but he tends to be a sort of lazy actor, doesn't he, if you don't push him?*
I don't know. When the picture was half over I said, 'You know, you're the biggest fraud I've ever met in all my life.' He grinned and said, 'Why?' I said, 'You pretend you don't care a damn thing about a scene, and you're the hardest-working so-and-so I've ever known.' He said, 'Don't tell anybody.' I think he's one of the best actors that I know. But I don't think Mitchum can carry a thing. He doesn't have anywhere near the force that Wayne has. As Wayne says, 'You give everybody else the fireworks, and I have to carry the damn thing.' That's about true.

How did the script of El Dorado *evolve from the novel by Harry Brown,* The Stars in Their Courses?
I bought a story that was a Greek tragedy, where everybody got killed. Leigh Brackett and I finished the first script. I read it and said, 'Hey, this is going to be one of the worst pictures I've ever made. I'm no good at this downbeat stuff.' She said, 'What do we do?' I said, 'Well, let's write a new one.' So we decided to keep one scene, and that's where Wayne shot the boy on top of the rock. One of the reasons we did it was because we felt that would start the picture off as a tragedy, and then we could turn it into fun. And we worked on it that way, and we were lucky working it out because we were working with characters instead of a story. The author of the book that we took it from was very angry because he said he thought it was a bunch of junk.

What's Leigh Brackett like to work with?
She wrote that like a man. She writes good.

Is it true that when you first read her stuff you thought she was a man because of her name?
Yeah. I hired her through an agent, and I thought I was hiring a man. We had *Big Sleep*, and Bill Faulkner wanted a job. Leigh

167

Brackett knew screen formula and a little bit about how to write scenes. They did the script for that in eight days. She wrote good.

In El Dorado *you dealt with a rather sophisticated sexual situation, Wayne and Mitchum both being involved with Charlene Holt. But it's very oblique who is involved with her at what point. I also had the feeling that she was supposed to be the madame of a house of prostitution, but you never really made that clear. Do you like to just suggest things like that?*
I like to do it the way we did it. I didn't intend her as being a madame. I just thought she was a normal girl. One guy walked off, and she slept with another one. Wayne comes to town, and she starts sleeping with him. They still remained friends. I'm just doing the way people really are. That's what happens in life. People liked it so much that the next story I've got [*When It's Hot Play It Cool*] is on the same basis, only carried a lot farther. I haven't done a story of two friends in love in a modern way with the same woman.

I think you are very modern in the sense that you deal with the kind of sexual relationships where people don't have long-term bonds. They're more pragmatic about it, which is one reason I think your films work well today. By doing it in a modern way, do you mean more explicit sexually?
A little franker. We touched on it in *El Dorado*.

Two men in love with the same woman is a situation which occurs in your films over and over again. Does that come out of your experience?
That's one of the simple rules of drama. It makes good scenes. If people that the audience like in a picture like somebody else, that's the best boost for a character that you can make. Now, if you've got a heavy liking someone, that's no boost for the person that they like. But when you've got a nice guy that likes someone, immediately that character is boosted.

It seems to me that the morality you deal with in your films is based more on the relationships between small groups of people than on

168

abstract codes of behaviour, like in the John Ford films, for example. Wayne in El Dorado *could be working for one side or another, and he has to get there before he makes up his mind. What motivates Wayne is his friendship for Mitchum and his debt to the family more than his judgment of what's going on in this range war. Do you agree?*

Very much so. I'm much more interested in the story of a friendship between two men than I am about a range war or something like that. There's probably no stronger emotion than friendship between men. When it comes to Wayne and his relationships, that's better than the story.

What makes someone a villain in your movies? There are certain kinds of characters who seem to deserve getting shot.

Oh, I don't know. I think Chris George in *El Dorado* was a pretty nice guy, wasn't he?

Yes, but why wouldn't you have him sent through the door to get shot as the Robert Donner character was? What's the difference? What kind of man do you consider a bad guy?

Anybody who frames somebody, to kill him. How would *you* feel if you were in there, and there was some guy framing *you*? You'd say, 'You son of a bitch, you're going to get what you were gonna do to me.' But Chris George said, 'You didn't give me a chance.' And Wayne said, 'You're too good to give a chance to.' That's their theory; that's their code, their religion.

Was the reference by the gunsmith to 'shoot the piano player' a conscious reference to Truffaut's film?

I don't remember.

The man who played the gunsmith is the man who painted those wonderful title paintings.

The man who played the gunsmith is the most famous American western painter today, Olaf Wieghorst. He's really good.

How do you feel about Rio Lobo?

I didn't think it was any good. I only made it because I had a damn

69 *Rio Lobo*: 'You don't quite think it's going to be a western.'

70 *Rio Lobo*: Wayne, Jennifer O'Neill and Jorge Rivero.

good story. We'd have had a good picture, but by that time the studio [Cinema Center Films] had mismanaged things so badly they couldn't afford to have another good actor in it with Wayne. So I threw out the story and wrote a new one quickly. I kept the story to do later [in *When It's Hot Play It Cool*]; I was going to use that story in *Rio Lobo*. A lot of pictures lack strength because they put all their money into one guy. When you want somebody that's expensive, they say, 'Couldn't you do it with somebody cheaper?' You don't actually save money by hiring somebody cheaper, it just takes you longer to shoot, and it isn't as good.

Did you think that Jorge Rivero would be strong enough before you hired him?
I thought so. He was a good-looking boy, and he was strong; he represented Mexico in the Olympic Games [of 1964, as a swimmer]. But in order to do anything, he had to think it in Spanish, and then transfer his lines mentally to English. He was really too slow, and he didn't have any authority at all.

How were the girls cast? Were there two or three girls in there who were forced on you?
We had a great girl, a German girl, but she wasn't allowed in by the Screen Actors Guild. They said, 'You could get somebody over here.' So I only had a few days to cast the part. The girl who played in it [Jennifer O'Neill] started to work fine, but she got a lead, and she thought she was a star. She came down on location with a nurse, two children, three dogs, and a husband that she was having a fight with. She couldn't afford to pay her hotel bill. Stupid dame. She had a chance to be good. She's such a beautiful girl, she should have done well. You see, I wouldn't have used a bunch of girls. We would have made the same scenes with one girl, but I didn't have anybody who was good enough to hold down all that stuff.

The Mexican girl [Susana Dosamantes] was pretty good.
The Mexican girl was *good*. I'm sorry that I didn't use her for the other part. It only needed a little bit to make it better, but I had to change *Rio Lobo*, so now I'm going to do that love story.

32

Hatari!

71 Hawks on location on *Red Line* 7000.

Hatari! was about a hunting season. It started with the beginning, the planning, and finished with the windup of the thing. It had a form of simplicity. There was just a group of people who were hunting for circuses and making money. The Indian [Bruce Cabot] got hit by a rhino in the very first part of the thing. That's a trick I use all the time. To make a business dangerous, you hurt somebody in the beginning. Flying, racing, anything, I always start with as much of a smash as I can. So it introduced people, and then you brought in another boy: they needed another one to help them. You just let it go. And if your story's like that it's fine, but if you've got individual plots like in *Red Line 7000*, then you're gone. That movie was no good. I was trying to do something, I tried an experiment. I had three good stories about the race track, but none of them would make a picture, so I thought maybe I can put them together. And just when I got people interested in two people, I cut over and started to work with two more, and when the audience got interested in them, I went over to two others, and pretty soon the audience got disgusted, and I got disgusted too. To be serious, I think there were some pretty good things in it, but as a piece of entertainment, I don't think I did a good job. I think there were some individual scenes that were pretty good, and there were a lot of great race scenes. But I'm not proud of the picture as a whole.

I was talking to Truffaut about Hatari! *the other day, and he made an interesting remark about it. His film* Day for Night *is about the making of a film. And he said he thought* Hatari! *was really a film about film-making and you used hunting as a metaphor for that. He said you were perhaps conscious of doing it, because John Wayne is like the director of a film. They sit around at night and write on a blackboard what they're going to do the next day, and he tells the crew how to do it, and then they all go out the next morning in a convoy of trucks, and it shows them staging these scenes. Then they come back and at night they go to the bar and relax just like a film crew on location.*

Probably had a lot to do with the thing, because there wasn't much story. I accept anything that anybody says about it. The Frenchmen are so funny. They attribute things. I can't even understand the

72 *Red Line 7000*: Marianna Hill as Gaby.

73 *Red Line 7000*: 'There were a lot of great race scenes.'

words that they use in talking about why you arrive at such a thing. There was quite a little discussion as to how to tell that damn story. We had so much to do that was good, because that thing kept going. The episodes were so good – the story actually wasn't as good as the episodes. And I was worried about casting. I thought of Stella Stevens. I thought that she had some promise at that time. And I thought of a blonde girl down in Africa, and I thought of Harlow in *Red Dust* [1932, directed by Victor Fleming]. And then I thought, 'Oh, God, I'm gonna throw this thing off to one side.' I worked on *Red Dust*. The thing that was interesting about that was making Gable a heavy. And every time we made a picture with Gable, if we were smart we made him a heavy, because he was such a likeable heavy. But in doing this thing I thought, 'Oh, I can't use a blonde, I've got to get a natural-looking girl.' I had met [Elsa] Martinelli before, and I knew she was a very natural-looking person. I didn't know whether her English was better, and I called her up, and she talked good English. I said, 'You go out and make a test and let me hear you talk on this thing.' I fixed her up with a cameraman, and she made a test and sent it back here, and I hired her. She was charming doing what she did. We took that part of the story from a real character, a German girl who was so damn good-looking that people put her in a position to get pictures. She was the best animal photographer in the world. So I stole the idea and used it. I didn't want any strange plots; this was a story about a bunch of people catching animals, and I wasn't going to mix it up with other things. Wayne was a fellow who had been burnt by a previous thing, and he wasn't going to have anything to do with a girl. She came in to take photographs. The Frenchman [Gérard Blain] came in to shoot. The German [Hardy Kruger] was in love with the daughter [Michèle Girardon] of the owner of the place. And Red Buttons was there to get some fun out of.

Clark Gable was supposed to have been in Hatari! *originally, wasn't he?*
We were gonna make it with Gable and Wayne. But Paramount was taken over just about that time by a lawyer [Jacob M. Karp], and he said, 'We haven't got enough money to get another leading man.'

What kind of parts would Wayne and Gable have played?
They would be the other two parts, the parts of the Frenchman and the German. They would make it a love story. They would both like the girl.

You mean they would have been rivals for the female photographer?
Yeah. But, you see, that picture, like *Rio Lobo*, was weakened by not having anybody that had any strength in there at all except Wayne. There wasn't anything there; it just became nothing. There was no fight; there was no argument.

Yet I can't think of any movie with a group of people whose company I more enjoy being in than Hatari!
Oh, I know it. I like to be around 'em too.

You told me that all the actors in Hatari! *did their own animal catching, including John Wayne.*
Yes, that's true. Wayne got himself into real trouble once in a while.

He got awfully close to that rhino.
Closer than I'd want to get, I'll tell you that.

How did you keep the rhino from smashing into the camera? The camera was on the truck itself, close to the ground.
He did pretty well; he knocked about three cameras off. But we had quite a few cameras around there, and they got the rest of it.

It's obvious that you couldn't control much of what happened. How did you prepare for the hunting scenes?
We had some marvellous camera cars – six months building, could do about eighty miles an hour right across the desert. They were all made specially, with aluminium frames, big motors that were fixed for that altitude, and they could keep up with about anything. They had to go awfully fast, because that old truck you saw there was the very latest thing in the world with an old body dropped on it. It had somewhere around twelve shock absorbers. You had to have them because that was pretty rough country. And we had a pretty

74 *Hatari!*: Chasing the rhino.

75 *Hatari!*: Wayne and Elsa Martinelli.

well-trained crew. We had three airplanes up there, and we had around fifty vehicles of various kinds, jeeps, trucks, station wagons, everything. They were all numbered with big numbers. I could talk to the airplanes, and I could talk to the cars. An airplane would say, 'Car 33 is headed for a good bunch of rhinos.' So I'd say, 'Where's Car 33?' They put up a flag, and we'd find out where 33 was, and we'd all head for 33. And then we'd hear a voice say, 'Be careful when you swing round that bunch of trees; they're right behind there, and they look kinda mean.' And then you'd hear, 'Look out there!' and a big crash, and the boys in the airplane would say, 'I *told* you they were mean.' Then we'd make a scene – we only had three or four minutes to make a scene. We had to catch them and get 'em into a cage. Three or four minutes was a long time, because they weren't fun. All those boys were really ad-libbing and everything. You probably got some of Wayne's. We succeeded in cutting out a few things that he said. I would yell to Wayne, 'Gobble!' and that meant I could put in anything afterwards I wanted to. The boys got very good at it; they'd turn around to one another and just say something, anything. I didn't care what they said. And we put the lines in afterwards. There was nothing you could write in a room that would work there. It was quite a job. I think we chased nine rhinos and caught four to get the scenes in this part of the picture. Almost every night we had a little conference where we would tell people what was dangerous and what they should watch out for. For instance, you could get up to a zebra behind, but if you got near his head, he'd bite. If you're gonna shoot an elephant, as he got closer to you you'd shoot lower because he was higher. We had skull practice all the time. Because when we started out in the morning, we never knew what we were gonna get. Ostrich, wild boar, wildebeest, lion, anything, we took 'em just as they came. It was a lot of fun. We had a stockade where we kept the animals, and when we left there we gave them to the government. We brought the baby elephants back here with us, and a hyena and a few things like that.

Didn't you give a couple of the animals to the Los Angeles Zoo?
Yeah. There are quite a few down in San Diego. And there's one

back in Indiana, because the governor found out I came from there, and so he ordered one.

33

Critics

Why do you think it took so long for you and other directors to be appreciated in America?
Well, they had these big companies and they didn't want *us* to get big because it cost them too much money. I like the French people. As a matter of fact, the French people are the first people who thought I was any good as a director, so naturally I would like them. Every time I go over to France I meet about thirty directors. We have a few drinks and talk. The last time I was over there, I said, 'You fellows get more ideas about my work. I enjoy listening to you, but where you get the ideas I don't know.' I said we're going to do a picture about two fellows next [*When It's Hot Play It Cool*], and the girl has been married to one of 'em and has fallen in love with the other. And they're still friends. In the end of the story, she walks out on both of them. They get drunk and sing their way home. It's a little South American town, no electric lights. Just two beds and the moonlight coming through a window. They undress, fall into the beds, only they land in the same bed. And one of 'em says, 'Bill, there's somebody in my bed.' And Bill says, 'Joe, there's somebody in mine too. What'll we do?' 'Well, Bill, you throw yours out; I'll throw mine out.' So there's a big fight. 'How'd you come out, Bill?' And he says, 'Mine threw me out.' 'OK, you can come and sleep with me.' And now I said, 'You Frenchmen are going to think that I've got a couple of homosexuals there.' They all laughed. And I said, 'That's about the way you're gonna interpret it.' No, they love to study this stuff. They know my pictures better than I do.

Well, what do you think when critics say, as some in fact have, that the male characters in your films border on homosexuality?
I'd say it's a goddam silly statement to make. It sounds like a

homosexual speaking. People attribute all kinds of meanings and everything. In one picture [*Tiger Shark*] a ship captain who was very jealous threw a man overboard to the sharks. And some woman asked me what kind of an action did I think that was. I said, 'Well, I don't know, somebody tried to kill somebody else.' She said, 'Would you approve of that?' And I said, 'Well, I don't know much else he could *do*. He couldn't have burned him up on board ship or anything, so he threw him over to the sharks.' I don't know. I don't know where those things come from. Well, I'll tell you about critics. I had a telephone call the other day from Dick Schickel. He made a show on me [in his TV documentary series] *The Men Who Made the Movies*. Dick said, 'I want to tell you that the thing I made with you is doing four times the business of any of the other ones.' I said, 'Thank you. That's very pleasant to hear.' 'But,' he said, 'I want to apologize. I didn't say anything about your comedies.' 'Well,' I said, 'Dick, that's par for the course. You're a critic, aren't you? Critics don't ever know when a thing's funny, so they don't want to talk about it.' *I* don't know why a thing is funny. It just happens to be funny, but the poor damn critic has to write about it. But, actually, very few critics, in my opinion, know what the hell it's all about. Some of them I think are very, very smart, but I don't pay any attention to most of them. When I made *The Big Sleep*, the studio wanted me to go back to New York and talk to the critics. We had a good lunch at 21, and I had to get up and speak. I said, 'I don't know really why we're here except that you fellows seem to like what you drink and what you eat and everything. But you're not going to like this picture much.' And they said, 'Why?' I said, 'Well, you like a picture that if a fellow's driving along and puts out his left hand, he turns left. If he puts out his hand to the right, he turns right. I didn't do any of those things in this picture. I don't think any of you are going to know what to say about it. It doesn't make any sense.' And they questioned me about it, and I said, 'Probably the only thing that's unusual about this is that the story is told without any red herrings. The audience knows exactly what happened. They know everything that Bogart knows. He's in on every scene, and the scene ends when he goes off.' I never got such good reviews of a picture in my life, because it gave them something to write about.

I'm afraid that is so. If you had to write a criticism of a picture every day, you'd get awful sick and tired of trying to figure out what to say about it.

76 *Man's Favorite Sport?*: Fishing . . .

77 *Man's Favorite Sport?*: . . . and chasing women.

78 *Man's Favorite Sport?*: Hawks directing Rock Hudson, Maria Perschy, and Paula Prentiss.

79 *Man's Favorite Sport?*: The completed scene.

34

Today's Actresses

There aren't as many good actresses today as there used to be.
You can count 'em on your fingers if you're down to one finger.

There are a lot of models around but not a lot of strong actresses.
There's no training for them. I don't know where they're gonna get
'em. You get a girl on a damn television series, and then they get
cute. I had Barbara Feldon come over, and I said, 'Look, I thought
you were going to be one of the best that I've ever seen, and then you
got cute. Here are two or three scenes. I want you to learn 'em, come
in and read 'em with me. And no being cute!' She was cute. Couldn't
use her. And she was good.

*When you say they need training, are you talking about theatrical
training?*
Studying, theatrical training, something like that. You see, a lot of
the girls used to be extra girls, and they became good. I don't think
they want to work today. I've tried a couple of the new people, but
the minute you say, 'You've got the part,' they stop working.

You're always looking for new actresses, aren't you?
Well, I don't see anybody or know anybody. But you get these girls
that have been in television, and oh, golly, they're awful. I watched
somebody doing a television show a while ago, and he said, 'All
right, let's make a take.' A couple of lines were kind of messed up. It
was very bad. 'Cut! Print it!' Oh, Christ! I said, 'Is that the way
you're making these pictures?' He said, 'That's the way you have to
make 'em. If we don't make them on time, we get fired.' Nobody
cares how good or bad they are or anything like that. They just get
'em done on time. Well, when people come out of that, what are you

gonna do? And you get 'em in, and you expect 'em to be as good as Katie Hepburn. I think that Paula Prentiss is good. She ought to be a big comedy star. I don't know what's the matter.

35

Today's Movies

You're quite an inspiration for a lot of young European directors. What do you think of their work?
A number of them have a great deal of talent, but they're telling pictures that are good for only France, Italy, and Germany. When I go over there I talk to them about it. I say, 'Why don't you fellows widen out, make a picture that is good for the world? You aren't going to get enough money to work with unless you can get it out of universal entertainment.' And I think that they're beginning to work on that. A couple of the Frenchmen do beautiful jobs, and I admire their work. Peter Bogdanovich is good. I think he's the best of all the young directors. Of the older directors, I admire Carol Reed's work very much. I like Hitchcock's work, and Billy Wilder's. When I think I can learn something, I go to see any of their pictures, but if I think I can't learn, I don't go.

You've directed a lot of very erotic scenes, such as in To Have and Have Not. *But what do you think of the new sexual explicitness in movies?*
Maybe I'm just getting old, but I don't think they're much good. So much of it's done in such bad taste. I did a picture with Cary Grant, *I Was a Male War Bride*, it's about as sensual a picture as you can make. But nobody resented it at all. Now I go out and see pictures where somebody's going to do sex as though it were in a burlesque house, and – it's hard to talk about that. I don't pay much attention to it. I think that the relationship between Bogart and Bacall was a good one. I think that if they'd do more of that type of relationship, they would do better with it, because it didn't come out and show what they were doing all the time.

You seem to have a desire to keep up with what's going on in the film business, to keep up with the trends.
Oh, yeah, but with a picture like *Walking Tall* or *Billy Jack*, all you think of is, 'It must be a nation of morons.' Then they make a good old-fashioned picture that people go to see. They seem to be doing good right now with things like *Airport* and – what's that ship thing? *The Poseidon Adventure*. And you know that's a lousy picture, but there must be something basic. It's the same kind of a basis that makes *Ben-Hur* popular every time they make it. They still go for a well-made picture. I thought *The Sting* was damn well-made. But, you know, strange movies are doing amazing business. That doesn't mean that they're great. You know that little picture that Max Baer made, *Macon County Line*?

You were helping him with the script, weren't you?
Yeah, and editing and everything. I wrote a letter and got him a release, and it grossed $10 million in the first six weeks. God knows it isn't so good. It isn't bad, but it isn't so good. This *Walking Tall* thing is making an amazing fortune.

Baer is going to direct his next film, isn't he?
Yeah, write it and direct it and probably act in it and everything. I don't think too much of the story. It's a story of an Irish family [*The McCullochs*]. He's relying on latrine jokes and Irish humour, that kind of stuff. I don't think it's too funny. But I only see a few pictures I like.

What did you think of The Godfather?
Well, listen, you ask me too much 'if that was good', you know. I don't *like* a lot of that stuff. Christ, *The Godfather* – I don't think it was as good as *Scarface*, and it was certainly taken scene after scene out of *Scarface*. I don't care. They're pretty smart. How are you going to say what stealing is? I steal as much as anybody, so I can't blame them. The only thing I don't like is to have them know what kind of a story I'm going to make. If I let anybody have a script, when I'm ready to shoot every agent in town will know that script better than I do and come over and talk about it. And you can't

possibly keep scenes from that from going into television and everything. So, for the last four or five years, I've had *two* scripts when I do a picture – one that I let people read, without a lot of the best stuff in it, and the other I keep for myself.

36

Late Projects

What's your next picture?
Well, I've got a couple of 'em. One's a crazy, wild comedy [*When It's Hot Play It Cool*] that goes over about six countries. It's about the oil business.

Isn't it actually a remake of A Girl in Every Port?
Not a remake, but I don't want to be sued or have some judge ask me where did I get my idea for the story, because I'd have to say from *Girl in Every Port*. So I bought it to make sure it would be OK.

What stage are you in the writing?
To be truthful, about three years ago [1971], we had finished a first treatment of the story, and then all this crazy junk started. I said to Wayne, 'I don't know what to make nowadays except westerns.' So I dropped that oil story until I could figure out what people really liked and what they wanted, because I didn't want to go to all the trouble of making a movie and having it turn out lousy. And the westerns made money, and I had fun doing 'em. Now I'm doing a complete rewrite on the oil story – not on the story, but just on the treatment of the thing. Everything is much funnier. Everything is made for comedy.

When do you expect to make it?
Soon as I can get six countries who are not fighting together – no kidding, it's really tough going today. I wanted to go to Djakarta. We used to be able to go to a studio and call up the location department and say, 'How is it for working in Djakarta?' 'Oh,' they'd say, 'it's fine, you do this, you do that.' Today you have to find out for yourself. Today I have to write a letter to the consul. The

consul there said, 'Bring bulletproof glass for your automobiles.' You throw out your whole sequence about Djakarta and put it some other place, then you find out whether you can work there. The only way is direct communication with somebody who's down there. I have a little connection with the oil business. So I use the oil companies to get my information. I send a letter to somebody that I know here, and he forwards it to Turkey. He says, 'What about coming down and making a picture?' They say, 'Stay away. They will lie, cheat, and blackmail you.' It's really tough going today. Saudi Arabia is not too happy to have us down there right now. A lot of them say, 'Wait till the present trouble clears up, and then we can tell you that you've got a few weeks in which you can work.' What I think we can do is that Pierre Schoendoerffer can take a French crew and go in there and get an awful lot of second-unit stuff, and they won't ever know anything about it. We'll just use a couple of doubles. Then we'll build the sets to match in with it down in Madrid. Schoendoerffer's a very brilliant guy. He made a film in Vietnam called *The Anderson Platoon* that won all kinds of kudos.

Didn't you want to make a film about the Vietnam War several years ago?
Yeah, I spent a lot of money on a Vietnam story that's a real good one. Then I decided I'd be wasting my time. It's sitting around – if somebody wants to buy it, I'll be glad to sell it to them. I wanted to find out first what kind of assistance I could get from the Army. It wasn't very much. They wanted to tell me how to make the picture, tell how to do the story. So I took a loss on that.

What was the plot?
I'm going to use it, but not in Vietnam.

Did it make any statement about the war?
I've *never* made a statement. Our job is to make entertainment. I don't give a God damn about taking sides.

In a situation like that, though, wouldn't it be hard not to make some kind of statement? Because it was such an emotional subject, it's hard not to take sides in some way even if you're just making a story about two guys. There are bound to be implications.

Oh, I don't know. You see, I don't look at it that way. I think they've gotten all mixed up. They've gotten so you can't have a Jewish comic because you're making fun of the Jews. You can't have an Irish comic because you're making fun of the Irish. There's more goddam *minorities*. Nasser banned a picture called *Land of the Pharaohs* because he said it made it seem as though a Jew designed the pyramids. It's hard enough to make movies without getting into all that stuff.

Do you have a cast in mind for the oil story?

Clint Eastwood and Steve McQueen have shown desire to play in this oil picture. But I tell you, some of these fellows – Eastwood makes so much money now that you'd stand a better chance without him. You can't afford to pay him so much money because you're competing against pictures that don't cost so much. You're better off using someone who isn't so expensive. I told 'em I wouldn't pay 'em, but I'd give them part of it, I'd split it. Eastwood said he wants to study the way I work. He said he's doing well enough now that he can afford to take a share of the picture. 'Anything that I lose won't hurt me,' he said. But every time I think about some of the scenes and how funny they are, and I think about those two guys in 'em, I get sick. Because neither of them is a bit funny. And I don't think that I can *make* them funny. Steve McQueen can't hold any more beer, and he's getting so heavy and fat, I wouldn't want him to work for me at all. I'd much rather get Starsky and Hutch [Paul Michael Glaser and David Soul] to do it. You understand we've got to find some new ones like Starsky and Hutch.

Eastwood actually has a funny side because he's so cold. But you wouldn't want him and McQueen together.

I've got an introduction scene of a fellow on an airplane. A place like Djakarta. Night. Plane stops, and people get on. A rather lush, good-looking girl sits in the seat beside him. The flight starts, and they go to sleep. And the girl's head falls over on his shoulder, her hair gets in his nose, her hand comes over and goes inside his shirt. He doesn't know quite what to do. The stewardess comes over and says, 'Fasten your seatbelts, please. You'd better fasten hers.' And he says, 'I don't know her.' The stewardess says, 'You don't know her?' And a guy says, '*I* do. I'm her husband.' That's how they meet. But, you see, you have to be careful who you get to play it. The girl is a good character. A little girl I call 'Rabbit', for obvious reasons. She just sails through life sleeping with everybody and enjoying the whole thing. I don't know who to get to play it. Could be very, very funny. Stella Stevens ten years ago probably would have been very good for it. But she's phony, you see. She isn't real. She's too blonde, you know what I mean? She's too cute. Like Marilyn Monroe.

What's your other project?
I expect to make a picture in Russia. They asked me to come over there, and I thought the American people would be very glad to see a picture that was made there. They've got a great cameraman over there, they've got good labs, and they've got good studios. I can go over there and make a movie. But I said, 'I understand you're difficult to get along with.' They said, 'What do you mean?' I said, 'Telling people how to make a picture.' They said, 'We wouldn't tell *you*.' I said 'OK,' and I told them a story that you might call pretty political. I didn't think they'd even touch it, and instead of that they seemed to be delighted. I said, 'Two Americans are trying to get away from the Russian police, and they go in the back door of the Ballet Russe. And then the cops come in, they're dancing in the chorus.' They started to laugh. I said, 'Then they go from there, and they get in with the National Symphony Orchestra.' They said, 'What do you want with them?' I said, 'I want them to do the score for the picture.' They said, 'OK. You can do anything you want.' So I asked for a certain cameraman that I've seen, and they said I could have him. I asked for an art director. I asked for everything I could think of. And they said, 'Come ahead.' They said they'd put up some money to make the picture if they can have the Russian rights. And I didn't say that if I didn't give it to 'em, they'd steal it, so I just let it go at that. I said, 'Now, look, it costs a lot of money to get ready, to get started, and I have to make deals, become responsible

for the picture. I'm going to send you a script, and I want every page of that script initialled in front of the American consul.' I still don't know if I'm going to have any trouble or not, but at the *thought* of any trouble – actually, they're very pleasant and very nice.

How did the project come about?
I went to the San Sebastian Film Festival. I was the president of the jury and was very careful not to inflict my things on the jury. They chose a picture called *The Glass House*, directed by Truman Capote. I said, 'I can't go along with you on that. I made it once better [*The Criminal Code*], and somebody made it better than I did, called *The Big House*. It's just old stuff. I'll go along with you if you give the Russian picture a special award.' The Russian people were very happy to get it, and the head of their delegation came to me afterward and said, 'You've been invited to come over and make a picture.' I said, 'Why is everybody so nice?' They said the fellow that's running Russia now, whoever he is, he loves westerns, and he thinks I make the best ones, so he wants me over there.

37

Advice to Young Directors

When young directors ask you for advice, what do you tell them?
[William] Friedkin was going around with my daughter in New York. He asked me how I liked his last picture, *The Boys in the Band*. I said, 'If you're going to be making pictures you'll have to learn not to ask that. I thought it was lousy.' He said, 'I'm not interested in why.' I said, 'It's too bad that somebody who has the talent you have should waste his time on junk like that.' He took it all very, very well. I said, 'You made another lousy picture before that called *The Night They Raided Minsky's*. You're gonna run out of pictures. They're not going to let you make them unless you make something that people want to see. And then they're gonna tell you how to make them.' And he said, 'Well, what kind of thing do you mean?' And I said, 'Do something that's entertaining. People seem to like chase scenes. Make a good chase. Make one better than anyone's done.' And he did it in *The French Connection*. Did a good job of it.

You mentioned that you had an excellent training ground in one-reel comedies. Is there any kind of training that young people can get into today? What would you recommend to young people interested in film-making?
I went over to USC, and they gave a luncheon for me and asked me to be an honorary member of their cinema society. I got up and said, 'For God's sake, keep it funny, because the most horrible thing in the world is a beginner thinking he can get so damn dramatic that he's gonna sway people and he's gonna make a crying scene that will make them weep.' I haven't made a crying scene in twenty years, unless to get laughs out of, where a girl has had a few drinks and is crying, like in *Rio Bravo*. I just don't believe in that kind of

dramatics. The audience has seen that stuff too many times. Go out and work about characters. Find out about what can happen, what they can do. Work to get everybody that you've got in the scenario a character. I'm trying to help a young fellow who I think will be very successful. He's got a story about five children trying to rescue a kidnapped boy. I'm not really working on it, but I'm having fun with it. And we've got five of the damnedest characters you've ever known in all your life. I said, 'How many children have you got?' And he said, 'Five.' I said, 'No, you haven't. You got one. They all act the same. They're all the same people. Why don't you have one be a bookworm and another one this and another one that.' So he's trying a whole rewrite. After about two more rewrites he'll get something out of it. Everything that the kids do goes with their characters. When you get through with 'em, you're gonna know each one of them. That's what I would advise. For God's sake, see if you can't get some fun out of it.

80 *Rio Lobo*: Hawks's last film.

Filmography

Howard Winchester Hawks was born on May 30, 1896, in Goshen, Indiana, to Frank and Helen Hawks. He had two brothers in the film business: Kenneth, a director who was killed in 1930 while filming an aviation scene; and William, an agent and producer who died in 1969. He had two sisters: Grace, who died of tuberculosis in 1927; and another who died in childhood of food poisoning. Hawks moved to Neenah, Wisconsin, at the age of two and to Pasadena, California, at the age of ten. He attended high school in Glendora, California and for one year at Throop Polytechnic Institute in Pasadena (where he previously had spent a year of elementary school); he also attended Phillips Exeter Academy in New Hampshire and Cornell University in New York, where he studied engineering. He served in the US Army Air Service in Texas during World War I. Hawks was married three times: to Athole Shearer Ward (sister of Norma Shearer) from 1928 to 1940; to Nancy (Slim) Gross from 1941 to 1948; and to Dee Hartford from 1953 to 1959. He had four children – David, Barbara, Kitty, and Gregg – and he adopted Peter Ward, the son of his first wife. He died on December 26, 1977, at his home in Palm Springs, California.

Hawks worked in the property department of Famous Players-Lasky Studio (then the production arm of Paramount) during vacations from Cornell in 1916 and 1917. In 1917, he directed several scenes in Marshall Neilan's *The Little Princess*, starring Mary Pickford and Zasu Pitts. After returning from military service in World War I and working as a race car driver, an aviator, and an airplane builder, he directed several short comedy films and independently produced a number of films for directors such as Neilan and Allan Dwan. He joined the story department of Paramount in 1922 and worked on the scripts of about sixty movies, usually without credit. Hoping to become a director, he moved to MGM in 1924 but left after a year in the story department to sign a directing contract with William Fox Studios. Hawks received writing credit on four features before becoming a director (see the Filmography), and he also worked, uncredited, on the scripts of all the films he directed.

Besides producing many of the films he directed, he also produced *Corvette K-225* (directed by Richard Rosson, 1943) and *The Thing from Another World* (directed by Christian Nyby, 1951). Hawks assisted Nyby with the direction of *The Thing*, without credit. Also without credit, he directed parts of three films before being replaced by other directors: *The Prizefighter and the Lady* (directed by W. S. Van Dyke, 1933), *Viva Villa!* (directed by Jack Conway, 1934), and *The Outlaw* (directed by Howard Hughes, 1940–43). Hawks claimed to have contributed to the script of *Underworld* (directed by Josef Von Sternberg, 1927) and to the scripts of four films directed by Victor Fleming: *Red Dust* (1932), *Captains Courageous* (1937), *Test Pilot* (1938), and *Gone with the Wind* (1939), although that claim was disputed by Fleming's frequent collaborator John Lee Mahin, who worked on the scripts of those four films.

Hawks's unrealized projects included *Sutter's Gold*, a former Sergei Eisenstein project at Universal which William Faulkner wrote for Hawks before James Cruze finally directed the film in 1936; *Gunga Din*, the Kipling tale filmed by George Stevens in 1939 after Hawks had prepared an earlier version of the script with Ben Hecht and Charles MacArthur; Ernest Hemingway's *The Sun Also Rises*, eventually filmed by Darryl F. Zanuck with Henry King directing in 1957; Hemingway's *For Whom the Bell Tolls*, filmed by Sam Wood in 1943; Ian Fleming's first James Bond novel, *Casino Royale*, filmed in 1967 by producer Charles K. Feldman and several directors; *The Dark Page*, Samuel Fuller's novel about journalism, adapted into screenplays for Hawks by Fuller and by Jules Furthman around 1946 but filmed by Phil Karlson in 1952 as *Scandal Sheet*; *Dreadful Hollow*, an original horror screenplay by Faulkner written for Hawks in the 1940s; *Battle Cry*, a World War II story by Hawks and Faulkner, with a 1943 Faulkner screenplay, cancelled by Warner Brothers for budget reasons (no relation to the later World War II novel by Leon Uris or the film version directed by Raoul Walsh); *The Black Door* (or *Stiletto*), a Cleve F. Adams mystery, adapted by Leigh Brackett, planned by Hawks from 1945 through 1951; *The Left Hand of God*, a 1951 Faulkner adaptation for Hawks of the book by William E. Barrett which was filmed by Edward Dmytryk in 1955; a story about the building of an airfield in China during World War II, which gave Hawks the idea for his 1955 film about the building of a pyramid in ancient Egypt, *Land of the Pharoahs*; *Bengal Tiger*, a Brackett script about a tiger hunt in India, planned as a John Wayne film to follow *Hatari!*; *Yukon Trail*, an adventure story for John Wayne and Dean Martin, planned in 1962; Cervantes' *Don Quixote*, with Cary Grant and Cantinflas; the story of Hemingway's World War II relationship with photographer Robert Capa; a film taking place during the Vietnam War; a story of two Americans in the USSR escaping the Russian police; a western with Cary Grant playing a consumptive dentist similar to Doc Holliday; and a loose remake of Hawks's 1928 silent film *A Girl in Every Port*, planned from 1971 through 1976 under the titles *Now, Mr Gus* and *When It's Hot Play It Cool*, with the characters changed from sailors to world-travelling oil riggers.

Hawks appeared in four documentaries on his work: *The Great Professional – Howard Hawks*, a 1967 BBC TV special with Peter Bogdanovich as interviewer; *Plimpton: Shootout at Rio Lobo*, a 1970 ABC TV special produced and directed by William Kronick, written by George Plimpton and Kronick, featuring Plimpton, John Wayne et al. on the set of *Rio Lobo*; *The Men Who Made the Movies: Howard Hawks*, a 1973 PBS special produced, directed, and written by Richard Schickel as part of his series on veteran Hollywood directors for WNET, New York; and *Ein Verdammt Gutes Leben* (*A Hell of a Good Life*), a 1978 West German film written and directed by Hans C. Blumenberg.

The credits for Hawks's films are drawn from Peter Bogdanovich's filmographies in *The Cinema of Howard Hawks* (1962), *Movie* (December 1962), and *Cahiers du Cinéma* (January 1963); *Howard Hawks*, by Jean-Claude Missiaen (1966); *Howard Hawks*, by Robin Wood (1968); *The American Movies Reference Book*, vol. 1, *The Sound Era*, ed. by Robert Mandel (1969); *The American*

Film Institute Catalogue: Feature Films 1921–30, ed. by Kenneth W. Munden; *Howard Hawks*, by Jean A. Gili (1971); *Focus on Howard Hawks*, ed. by Joseph McBride (1972); and other sources.

FILMS AS WRITER (INCOMPLETE LIST)

1923
Quicksands (American Releasing Corp.)
Production Company: Agfar Corp.
Producer: Howard Hawks.
Director: Jack Conway.
Story: Hawks.
Photography: Harold Rosson, Glen MacWilliams.
Running time: 6–7 reels.
Released February 28, 1923, by the American Releasing Corp. Rereleased May 21, 1927, by Paramount Famous Lasky Corp., with a running time of 5 reels.
Cast: Helene Chadwick (The Girl), Richard Dix (1st Lieutenant), Alan Hale (Ferrago), Noah Beery ('Silent' Krupz), J. Farrell MacDonald (Col. Patterson), George Cooper (Matt Patterson), Tom Wilson (Sgt. Johnson), Dick Sutherland (Cupid), Hardee Kirkland (Farrell), Louis King (barfly), Jean Hersholt, Walter Long, Jack Curtis, William Dyer, Frank Campeau, Edwin Stevens, James Marcus, Lionel Belmore (members of dope ring).

A US Army lieutenant hunting dope smugglers along the Mexican border tries to rescue his girlfriend from the dope ring, but she is actually a secret agent, and the Army comes to the rescue.

1924
Tiger Love (Paramount)
Production Company: Famous Players-Lasky.
Producers: Adolph Zukor, Jesse L. Lasky.
Director: George Melford.
Script: Howard Hawks, adapted by Julie Herne, from the opera *El Gato Montes* by Manuel Peñella.
Photography: Charles G. Clarke.

Running time: 6 reels.

Released June 30, 1924, by Paramount Pictures.

Cast: Antonio Moreno (The Wildcat), Estelle Taylor (Marcheta), G. Raymond Nye (El Pezuno), Manuel Camero (Don Ramon), Edgar Norton (Don Victoriano Fuentes), David Torrence (Don Miguel Castelar), Snitz Edwards (The Hunchback), Monte Collins (Father Zaspard).

The Wildcat, a Spanish Robin Hood, abducts a wealthy girl on her wedding day and reveals that he is actually an aristocrat.

1925
The Dressmaker From Paris (Paramount)

Production Company: Famous Players-Lasky.

Producers: Adolph Zukor, Jesse L. Lasky.

Director: Paul Bern.

Script: Adelaide Heilbron, from a story by Heilbron and Howard Hawks.

Running time: 8 reels.

Released March 30, 1925, by Paramount Pictures.

Cast: Leatrice Joy (Fifi), Ernest Torrence (Angus McGregor), Allan Forrest (Billy Brent), Mildred Harris (Joan McGregor), Lawrence Gray (Allan Stone), Charles Crockett (mayor), Rosemary Cooper (mayor's daughter), Spec O'Donnell (Jim).

A midwestern soldier falls in love with a French girl in World War I, and she later turns up in his home town as a fashion designer in the clothing store he manages.

1926
Honesty – The Best Policy (Fox)

Production Company: Fox Film Corp.

Producer: William Fox.

Director: Chester Bennett, with additional sequence directed by Albert Ray.

Script: L. G. Rigby, from a story by Howard Hawks.

Photography: Ernest G. Palmer.

Running time: 5 reels.

Released August 8, 1926, by Fox.

Cast: Rockliffe Fellowes (Nick Randall), Pauline Starke (Mary Kay), Johnnie Walker (Robert Dore/author), Grace Darmond (Lily), Mickey Bennett (freckled boy), Mack Swain (Bendy Joe), Albert Gran (publisher), Dot Farley (author's wife), Heinie Conklin (piano player).

An author's wife threatens to send him to work unless he sells a story, so he concocts wild tales about their past.

FILMS AS DIRECTOR (SILENT)

1926
The Road to Glory (Fox)

Production Company: Fox Film Corp.
Executive Producer: William Fox.
Director: Howard Hawks.
Script: L. G. Rigby, from a story by Hawks.
Photography: Joseph August.
Running time: 6 reels.
Released (tinted) February 7, 1926, by Fox.
Cast: May McAvoy (Judith Allen), Leslie Fenton (David Hale), Ford Sterling (James Allen), Rockliffe Fellowes (Del Cole), Milla Davenport (Aunt Selma), John MacSweeney (butler), Hank (a dog).

Blinded in an auto accident which killed her father, a girl breaks with her fiancé, renounces God, and lives in the mountains. When the fiancé is injured by a falling tree, she prays, and his health and her sight are restored. (No print exists of this film. In 1936, Hawks made an unrelated film with the same title.)

1926
Fig Leaves (Fox)

Production Company: Fox Film Corp.
Producer: William Fox.
Production Supervisor: Winfield R. Sheehan.
Director: Howard Hawks.
Script: Hope Loring, Louis D. Lighton, from a story by Hawks.

Photography: Joseph August (two sequences in Technicolor).
Art Directors: William S. Darling, William Cameron Menzies.
Assistant Director: James Tinling.
Costumes: Adrian.
Editor: Rose Smith.
Titles: Malcolm Stuart Boylan.
Running time: 7 reels.
Released August 22, 1926, by Fox.
Cast: George O'Brien (Adam Smith), Olive Borden (Eve Smith), Phyllis Haver (Alice Atkins), Andre de Beranger (Josef Andre), William Austin (Andre's assistant), Heinie Conklin (Eddie McSwiggen), Eulalie Jensen (Madame Griswald).

After a prologue in Eden, with Eve telling Adam that she has 'nothing to wear', the same actors appear as a modern New York couple, a plumber and a fashion model, who stray to other partners but are reunited in the end.

1927
The Cradle Snatchers (Fox)
Production Company: Fox Film Corp.
Producer: William Fox.
Director: Howard Hawks.
Script: Sarah Y. Mason, from a play by Russell G. Medcraft and Norma Mitchell.
Photography: L. William O'Connell.
Assistant Director: James Tinling.
Titles: Malcolm Stuart Boylan.
Running time: 7 reels.
Released May 28, 1927, by Fox.
Cast: Louise Fazenda (Susan Martin), Ethel Wales (Ethel Drake), Dorothy Phillips (Kitty Ladd), J. Farrell MacDonald (George Martin), Franklin Pangborn (Howard Drake), William Davidson (Roy Ladd), Joseph Striker (Joe Valley), Nick Stuart (Henry Winton), Arthur Lake (Oscar), Dione Ellis (Ann Hall), Sammy Cohen (Ike Ginsberg), Tyler Brook (osteopath), Sally Eilers, Arthur Walis.

To cure their flirtatious husbands, three wives arrange with college boys to flirt with them at a party, and the husbands arrive with flappers in tow.

1927
Paid to Love (Fox)
Production Company: Fox Film Corp.
Producer: William Fox.
Director: Howard Hawks.
Script: William M. Conselman, Seton I. Miller, adapted by Benjamin Glazer from a story by Harry Carr.
Photography: L. William O'Connell.
Art Director: William S. Darling.
Editor: Ralph Dixon.
Assistant Director: James Tinling.
Titles: Malcolm Stuart Boylan.
Running time: 7 reels.
Released (tinted) July 23, 1927, by Fox.
Cast: George O'Brien (Crown Prince Michael), Virginia Valli (Gaby), J. Farrell MacDonald (Peter Roberts), Thomas Jefferson (King), William Powell (Prince Eric), Marta Sterling (maid), Hank Mann (servant).

An American banker befriends the crown prince of a Balkan kingdom and finds him a wife in an apache café.

1928
A Girl in Every Port (Fox)
Production Company: Fox Film Corp.
Producer: William Fox.
Director: Howard Hawks.
Script: Seton I. Miller, Reginald Morris, James Kevin McGuinness, from a story by Hawks.
Photography: L. William O'Connell, Rudolph Berquist.
Art Director: William S. Darling.
Assistant Director: Sidney Lanfield.
Costumes: Kathleen Dax.

Editor: Ralph Dixon.
Titles: Malcolm Stuart Boylan.
Running time: 6 reels.
Released (tinted) February 26, 1928, by Fox.
Cast: Victor McLaglen (Spike Madden), Robert Armstrong (Bill, called 'Salami'), Louise Brooks (Marie, called 'Mlle Godiva'), Myrna Loy (Jetta), Maria Casajuana (Chiquita), Gladys Brockwell (Madame Flore), Sally Rand (girl in Bombay), William Demarest (man in Bombay), Natalie Joyce, Dorothy Mathews, Elena Durado (girls in Panama), Francis McDonald (gang leader), Phalba Morgan (Lena, girl in Holland), Felix Valle (Lena's husband), Greta Yoltz (girl in Holland), Leila Hyams (the sailor's wife), Natalie Kingston (girl in South Sea islands), Caryl Lincoln (girl from Liverpool), Michael Visaroff.

Hawks's first 'love story between two men', about two sailors who share the same girlfriends in various ports of call but finally renounce women and go off together. (Hawks planned a loose remake of this film in the early 1970s under the titles *Now, Mr Gus* and *When It's Hot Play It Cool*, but the film was never made.)

1928
Fazil (Fox)
Production Company: Fox Film Corp.
Producer: William Fox.
Director: Howard Hawks.
Script: Seton I. Miller, Philip Klein, from the play *L'Insoumise*, by Pierre Frondale, and his English adaptation, *Prince Fazil*.
Photography: L. William O'Connell.
Assistant Director: James Tinling.
Editor: Ralph Dixon.
Running time: 113 minutes.
Released, with musical score and synchronized sound effects, June 4, 1928, by Fox.
Cast: Charles Farrell (Prince Fazil), Greta Nissen (Fabienne), John Boles (John Clavering), Mae Busch (Helene Debreuze), Vadim Uraneff (Ahmed), Tyler Brooks (Jacques Debreuze), Eddie Sturgis

(Rice), Josephine Borio (Aicha), John T. Murray (gondolier), Erville Anderson (Iman Idris), Dale Fuller (Zoureya), Hank Mann (Ali).

An Arab chieftan marries a Parisienne, but she rebels at her life in the desert, and they both die as a result of their quarrel.

1928
The Air Circus (Fox; part talking)
Production Company: Fox Film Corp.
Producer: William Fox.
Director: Howard Hawks, with dialogue scenes directed by Lewis R. Seiler.
Dialogue Director: Charles Judels.
Script: Seton I. Miller, Norman Z. McLeod, from a story by Graham Baker and Andrew Bennison.
Titles: William Kernell.
Dialogue: Hugh Herbert.
Photography: Dan Clark.
Assistant Director: William Tummell.
Editor: Ralph Dixon.
Running time: 118 minutes.
Released, with music and synchronized sound effects (and some dialogue scenes), September 30, 1928, by Fox.
Cast: Arthur Lake (Speed Doolittle), David Rollins (Buddy Blake), Sue Carol (Sue Manning), Louise Dresser (Mrs Blake), Charles Delaney (Charles Manning), Heinie Conklin (Jerry McSwiggin), Earl Robinson (Lt Blake).

Two young men at flying school overcome their fear and reckless-ness in the air with the help of a pretty aviatrix. (No print exists of this film.)

1929
Trent's Last Case (Fox)
Production Company: Fox Film Corp.
Producer: William Fox.
Production Supervisor: Bertram Millhauser.
Director: Howard Hawks.

Script: Scott Darling, adapted by Beulah Marie Dix, from the novel by E. C. Bentley.
Photography: Harold Rosson.
Assistant Director: E. D. Leshin.
Titles: Malcolm Stuart Boylan.
Running time: 96 minutes.
Released, with music and synchronized sound effects, March 31, 1929, by Fox.
Cast: Donald Crisp (Sigsbee Manderson), Raymond Griffith (Philip Trent), Raymond Hatton (Joshua Cupples), Marceline Day (Evelyn Manderson), Lawrence Gray (Jack Marlowe), Nicholas Soussanin (Martin), Anita Garvin (Ottilie Dunois), Edgar Kennedy (Inspector Murch).

A murder mystery about a man who commits suicide in such a way as to cast doubt on his wife and his secretary, who loves her. (Released only in England. Remade in England in 1953, directed by Herbert Wilcox.)

FILMS AS DIRECTOR (SOUND)

1930
The Dawn Patrol (Warner Bros.)
Production Company: First National Pictures.
Producer: Robert North.
Director: Howard Hawks.
Script: Hawks, Dan Totheroh, Seton I. Miller, from the story 'The Flight Commander', by John Monk Saunders.
Director of Photography: Ernest Haller.
Music: Leo F. Forbstein.
Art Director: Jack Okey.
Editor: Ray Curtis.
Aerial Advisor: Leo Nomis.
Running time: 95 minutes.
Released July 10, 1930, by Warner Bros.
Cast: Richard Barthelmess (Dick Courtney), Douglas Fairbanks, Jr. (Douglas Scott), Neil Hamilton (Major Brand), William Janney

(Gordon Scott), James Finlayson (field sergeant), Clyde Cook (Bott), Gardner James (Ralph Hollister), Edmund Breon (Lt Bathurst), Frank McHugh (Flaherty), Jack Ackroyd, Harry Allen (mechanics), Howard Hawks (stunt pilot).

The conflicts and loyalties among a group of doomed British World War I aviators. (Saunders won Academy Award for best original story. The film was retitled *Flight Commander* when the remake directed by Edmund Goulding appeared in 1938, with aerial footage taken from the Hawks version.)

1931
The Criminal Code (Columbia)
Production Company: Columbia.
Producer: Harry Cohn.
Director: Howard Hawks.
Script: Seton I. Miller, Fred Niblo, Jr, from a story by Martin Flavin.
Directors of Photography: James Wong Howe, L. William O'Connell.
Second Cameraman: Ted Tetzlaff.
Editor: Edward Curtiss.
Running time: 97 minutes.
Released January 15, 1931, by Columbia.
Cast: Walter Huston (Warden Brady), Phillips Holmes (Robert Graham), Constance Cummings (Mary Brady), Mary Doran (Gertrude Williams), De Witt Jennings (Gleason), John Sheehan (McManus), Boris Karloff (Galloway), Otto Roffman (Fales), Clark Marshall (Runch), Arthur Hoyt (Nettleford), Ethel Wales (Katie), John St Polis (Dr Rinewulf), Paul Porcasi (Spelvin), Hugh Walker (Lew), Jack Vance (reporter), Nicholas Soussanin, James Guilfoyle, Lee Phelps.

A tough district attorney becomes warden of a prison, and a convict falls in love with his daughter.

1932
Scarface, Shame of a Nation (United Artists-Atlantic)
Production Company: Hughes Productions.

Producers: Howard Hughes, Howard Hawks.

Director: Hawks.

Script: Ben Hecht, Seton I. Miller, John Lee Mahin, W. R. Burnett, Fred Pasley, from the novel by Armitage Trail.

Directors of Photography: Lee Garmes, L. William O'Connell.

Art Director: Harry Olivier.

Editor: Edward Curtiss, supervised by Douglas Biggs.

Assistant Director: Richard Rosson.

Music: Adolph Tandler, Gustav Arnheim.

Sound: William Snyder.

Running time: 90 minutes.

Released April 9, 1932, by United Artists-Atlantic Pictures. Rereleased in 1979 by Universal.

Cast: Paul Muni ('Scarface' Tony Camonte), Ann Dvorak (Cesca), Karen Morley (Poppy), Osgood Perkins (Johnny Lovo), Boris Karloff (Tom Gaffney), C. Henry Gordon (Ben Guarino), George Raft (Guino Rinaldo), Purnell Pratt (publisher), Vince Barnett (Angelo), Inez Palange (Mrs Camonte), Harry J. Vejar (Louie Costillo), Edwin Maxwell (chief of detectives), Tully Marshall (managing editor), Henry Armetta (Pietro), Maurice Black (hood), Bert Starkey (Epstein), Paul Fix (Gaffney hood), Hank Mann (worker), Charles Sullivan, Harry Tenbrook (bootleggers), John Lee Mahin (MacArthur of the *Tribune*), Howard Hawks (man in hospital bed).

The rise and fall of Chicago ganglord 'Scarface' Tony Camonte. (Filmed in 1930, but not released until 1932 because of censorship problems which necessitated partial reshooting.)

1932
The Crowd Roars (Warner Bros.)

Production Company: Vitaphone.

Producer: Bryan Foy.

Director: Howard Hawks.

Script: Kubec Glasmon, John Bright, Seton I. Miller, Niven Busch, from a story by Hawks.

Director of Photography: Sid Hickox.

Editors: John Stumar, Thomas Pratt.
Art Director: Jack Okey.
Music: Leo F. Forbstein.
Automotive Advisor: Fred Jackman.
Running time: 85 minutes.
Released April 16, 1932, by Warner Bros.
Cast: James Cagney (Joe Greer), Eric Linden (Eddie Greer), Joan Blondell (Ann), Ann Dvorak (Lee Merrick), Guy Kibbee (Dad Greer), Frank McHugh (Spud Connors), Billy Arnold (Bill), Leo Nomis (Jim), Charlotte Merriam (Mrs Connors), Harry Hartz, Ralph Hepburn, Fred Guisso, Phil Pardee, Spider Matlock, Jack Brisko, Fred Frame, Leo Norris, Dick Jones, Louis Meyer, Mel Kenaly (race drivers).

A race-car driver becomes jealous of his younger brother's success with fast cars and women. (Remade as *Indianapolis Speedway* by Lloyd Bacon in 1939, using racing footage from the Hawks film.)

1932
Tiger Shark (Warner Bros.)

Production Company: First National Pictures-Vitaphone.
Producer: Bryan Foy.
Director: Howard Hawks.
Script: Wells Root (and John Lee Mahin, uncredited), from *Tuna*, by Houston Branch.
Director of Photography: Tony Gaudio.
Assistant Director: Richard Rosson.
Editor: Thomas Pratt.
Music: Leo F. Forbstein.
Art Director: Jack Okey.
Costumes: Orry-Kelly.
Fishing Consultant: Capt. Guy Silva.
Running time: 80 minutes.
Released September 24, 1932, by Warner Bros.
Cast: Edward G. Robinson (Mike Mascarenas), Richard Arlen (Pipes Boley), Zita Johann (Quita Silva), Leila Bennett (Muggsy), Vince Barnett (Fishbone), J. Carroll Naish (Tony), William Ricciardi

(Manuel Silva).

A tuna fisherman whose arm has been severed by a shark marries a young woman and goes mad when he learns that she has fallen in love with his best friend.

1933
Today We Live (MGM)
Production Company: Metro-Goldwyn-Mayer.
Producer: Howard Hawks.
Director: Hawks.
Script: William Faulkner, Edith Fitzgerald, Dwight Taylor, from Faulkner's story 'Turn About'.
Director of Photography: Oliver T. Marsh.
Editor: Edward Curtiss.
Running time: 113 minutes.
Released March 3, 1933, by MGM.
Cast: Joan Crawford (Diana), Gary Cooper (Bogard), Robert Young (Claude), Franchot Tone (Ronnie), Roscoe Karns (McGinnis), Louise Closser Hale (Applegate), Rollo Lloyd (major), Hilda Vaughn (Eleanor).

A blinded torpedo boat pilot in World War I France embarks on a suicidal mission so that his girlfriend will be free to rejoin the man she really loves.

1934
Twentieth Century (Columbia)
Production Company: Columbia.
Producer: Howard Hawks.
Director: Hawks.
Script: Ben Hecht, Charles MacArthur, from their play, based on the play *Napoleon on Broadway*, by Charles Bruce Milholland.
Director of Photography: Joseph August.
Second Cameraman: Joseph Walker.
Editor: Gene Havlick.
Assistant Director: C. C. Coleman.
Running time: 91 minutes.

Released May 11, 1934, by Columbia.

Cast: John Barrymore (Oscar Jaffe), Carole Lombard (Mildred Plotka/Lily Garland), Walter Connolly (Oliver Webb), Roscoe Karns (Owen O'Malley), Charles Levison (Max Jacobs), Etienne Girardot (Matthew J. Clark), Dale Fuller (Sadie), Ralph Forbes (George Smith), Billie Seward (Anita), Clifford Thompson (Lockwood), James P. Burtis (conductor), Gigi Parrish (Schultz), Edgar Kennedy (McGonigle), Edward Gargan (sheriff), Snowflake (porter), Herman Bing (first beard), Lee Kohlmar (second beard), Pat Flaherty (Flannigan), Mary Jo Matthews (Emmy Lou), Fred Kelsey (detective on train), Cliff Thompson (Lockwood), Ky Robinson (detective), Nick Copeland (treasurer), Howard Hickman (Dr Johnson), Arnold Gray (stage actor), James Burke (Chicago detective), George Reed (Uncle Remus), Anita Brown (stage show girl), Irene Thompson (stage actress), Buddy Williams (stage actor), Clarence Geldert (Southern colonel), Lillian West (charwoman), Gaylord 'Steve' Pendleton (brother in play), George Offerman Jr (page boy), Frank Marlowe (stage carpenter), Lynton Brent (train secretary), Harry Semels (artist), King Mojave (McGonigle's assistant).

An egotistical theatrical producer pitches woo to a dizzy girl on the Twentieth Century Limited train between Chicago and New York City.

1935
Barbary Coast (United Artists)
Production Company: Goldwyn Productions.
Producer: Samuel Goldwyn.
Director: Howard Hawks.
Script: Ben Hecht, Charles MacArthur.
Director of Photography: Ray June.
Music: Alfred Newman.
Art Director: Richard Day.
Costumes: Omar Kiam.
Editor: Edward Curtiss.
Assistant Director: Walter Mayo.

Running time: 91 minutes.

Released September 27, 1935, by United Artists.

Cast: Miriam Hopkins (Mary Rutledge), Edward G. Robinson (Louis Chamalis), Joel McCrea (James Carmichael), Walter Brennan (Old Atrocity), Frank Craven (Col Marcus Aurelius Cobb), Brian Donlevy (Knuckles), Harry Carey (Slocum), Clyde Cook (Oakie), J. M. Kerrigan (Judge Harper), Donald Meek (McTavish), Roger Gray (Sandy), Rollo Lloyd (Wigham), Matt McHugh (Bronco), Otto Hoffman (Peebes), Fred Vogeding (captain), Cyril Thornton (steward), Dave Wengren (quartermaster), Anders von Haden (McCreaty), Jules Cowles (pilot), David Niven (Cockney sailor).

A Southern woman's rise and fall in San Francisco's infamous Barbary Coast underworld as the mistress of a gang leader.

1936
Ceiling Zero (Warner Bros.)

Production Company: Cosmopolitan Pictures–First National.

Producer: Harry Joe Brown.

Director: Howard Hawks.

Script: Frank Wead, from his play.

Director of Photography: Arthur Edeson.

Music: Leo F. Forbstein.

Art Director: John Hughes.

Editor: William Holmes.

Running time: 95 minutes.

Released January 25, 1936, by Warner Bros.

Cast: James Cagney (Dizzy Davis), Pat O'Brien (Jake Lee), June Travis (Tommy Thomas), Stuart Erwin (Texas Clark), Isabel Jewell (Lou Clark), Henry Wadsworth (Tay Lawson), Barton MacLane (Al Stone), Martha Tibbetts (Mary Lee), Craig Reynolds (Joe Allen), James H. Bush (Buzz Gordon), Robert Light (Les Bogan), Addison Richards (Fred Adams), Carlyle Moore, Jr (Eddie Payson), Richard Purcell (Smiley Johnson), Gordon 'Bill' Elliott (transportation agent), Pat West (Baldy Wright), Edward Gargan (Doc Wilson), Garry Owen (Mike Owens), Mathilde Comont (Mama Gini), Carol Hughes (Birdie), Frank Tomick, Paul Mantz (stunt fliers).

A mail pilot embarks on a suicidal flight in the fog after another pilot has crashed while taking his place.

1936
The Road to Glory (Twentieth Century-Fox)
Production Company: Twentieth Century-Fox.
Producers: Darryl F. Zanuck, Nunnally Johnson.
Director: Howard Hawks.
Script: Joel Sayre, William Faulkner, from the film *Les Croix de Bois*, by Raymond Bernard, and the novel by Roland Dorgelès.
Director of Photography: Gregg Toland.
Art Director: Hans Peters.
Music: Louis Silvers.
Set Decorator: Thomas Little.
Assistant Director: Edward O'Fearna.
Costumes: Gwen Wakeling.
Editor: Edward Curtiss.
Running time: 95 minutes.
Released June 2, 1936, by Twentieth Century-Fox.
Cast: Fredric March (Lt Michel Denet), Warner Baxter (Capt Paul Laroche), Lionel Barrymore (Papa Laroche), June Lang (Monique), Gregory Ratoff (Bouffiou), Victor Kilian (Régnier), Paul Stanton (relief captain), John Qualen (Duflous), Julius Tannen (Lt Tannen), Theodore Von Eltz (major), Paul Fix (Rigaud), Leonid Kinsky (Ledoux), Jacques Lory (courier), Jacques Vernaire (doctor), Edythe Taynore (nurse), George Warrington (old soldier).

An unpopular French Army officer in World War I dies and is replaced by his rival. (Unrelated except by title to Hawks's 1926 silent film.)

1936
Come and Get It (United Artists)
Production Company: Goldwyn Productions.
Producers: Samuel Goldwyn, Merritt Hulburd.
Directors: Howard Hawks, William Wyler.
Second-Unit Directors: Richard Rosson, Ross Lederman.

Script: Jules Furthman, Jane Murfin, from the novel by Edna Ferber.
Directors of Photography: Gregg Toland, Rudolph Maté.
Music: Alfred Newman.
Editor: Edward Curtiss.
Running time: 105 minutes.
Released October 29, 1936, by United Artists.
Cast: Edward Arnold (Barney Glasgow), Joel McCrea (Richard Glasgow), Frances Farmer (Lotta Morgan/Lotta Bostrom), Walter Brennan (Swan Bostrom), Andrea Leeds (Evvie Glasgow), Frank Shields (Tony Schwerke), Mady Christians (Karie), Mary Nash (Emma Louise Glasgow), Clem Bevans (Gunnar Gallagher), Edwin Maxwell (Sid LeMaire), Cecil Cunningham (Josie), Harry Bradley (Gubbins), Rollo Lloyd (Steward), Charles Halton (Hewitt), Phillip Cooper (chore boy), Al K. Hall (Goodnow), Robert Lowery (young man), Leoncie Rouy-Dementis.

The saga of a lumber baron and his rivalry with his son over the daughter of a woman he almost married. (Completed by William Wyler after Hawks was fired by Goldwyn. Reissued under the title *Roaring Timber.* Walter Brennan won Academy Award for best supporting actor.)

1938
Bringing Up Baby (RKO)
Production Company: RKO Radio Pictures.
Producer: Howard Hawks.
Associate Producer: Cliff Reid.
Director: Hawks.
Script: Dudley Nichols, Hagar Wilde, from a story by Wilde.
Director of Photography: Russell Metty.
Art Directors: Van Nest Polglase, Perry Ferguson.
Set Decorator: Darrell Silvera.
Costumes: Howard Greer.
Assistant Director: Edward Donahue.
Music: Roy Webb.
Editor: George Hively.
Running time: 102 minutes.

Released February 18, 1938, by RKO.
Cast: Cary Grant (David Huxley), Katharine Hepburn (Susan), Charles Ruggles (Major Horace Applegate), Walter Catlett (Constable Slocum), Barry Fitzgerald (Gogarty), May Robson (Aunt Elizabeth), Fritz Feld (Dr Lehmann), Leona Roberts (Mrs Hannah Gogarty), George Irving (Peabody), Tala Birrell (Mrs Lehmann), Virginia Walker (Alice Swallow), John Kelly (Elmer), Jack Carson (roustabout), Richard Lane (circus manager), Ward Bond (motorcycle cop), George Humbert (Louis, the headwaiter), Ernest Cossart (Joe, the bartender), Stan Blystone (porter), Asta (George, the dog), Nissa (Baby, the leopard).

A society girl's pet leopard buries the intercostal clavicle of a dinosaur skeleton, and a palaeontologist goes frantic looking for it.

1939
Only Angels Have Wings (Columbia)
Production Company: Columbia.
Producer: Howard Hawks.
Director: Hawks.
Script: Jules Furthman, from a story by Hawks.
Director of Photography: Joseph Walker.
Aerial Photographer: Elmer Dyer.
Music: Dimitri Tiomkin.
Art Director: Lionel Banks.
Costumes: Kalloch.
Editor: Viola Lawrence.
Running time: 121 minutes.
Released May 25, 1939, by Columbia.
Cast: Cary Grant (Geoff Carter), Jean Arthur (Bonnie Lee), Richard Barthelmess (Bat McPherson), Rita Hayworth (Judith McPherson), Thomas Mitchell (Kid Dabb), Sig Ruman (The Dutchman), Victor Kilian (Sparks), John Carroll (Gent Shelton), Allyn Joslyn (Les Peters), Donald Barry (Tex Gordon), Noah Beery, Jr (Joe Souther), Melissa Sierra (Lily), Lucio Villegas (Dr Lagorio), Forbes Murray (Hartwood), Maciste (guitar player), James Millican.

The physical and emotional hazards of flying mail planes over the Andes.

1940
His Girl Friday (Columbia)
Production Company: Columbia.
Producer: Howard Hawks.
Director: Hawks.
Script: Charles Lederer (and Ben Hecht, uncredited), from the play *The Front Page*, by Hecht and Charles MacArthur.
Director of Photography: Joseph Walker.
Art Director: Lionel Banks.
Costumes: Kalloch.
Music: Morris W. Stoloff.
Editor: Gene Havlick.
Running time: 92 minutes.
Released January 18, 1940, by Columbia.
Cast: Cary Grant (Walter Burns), Rosalind Russell (Hildy Johnson), Ralph Bellamy (Bruce Baldwin), Gene Lockhart (Sheriff Hartwell), Porter Hall (Murphy), Ernest Truex (Bensiger), Cliff Edwards (Endicott), Clarence Kolb (mayor), Roscoe Karns (McCue), Frank Jenks (Wilson), Regis Toomey (Sanders), Abner Biberman (Diamond Louie), Frank Orth (Duffy), John Qualen (Earl Williams), Helen Mack (Mollie Malloy), Alma Kruger (Mrs Baldwin), Billy Gilbert (Silas F. Pinkus), Pat West (Coaley), Edwin Maxwell (Dr Egelhoffer).

A tough female reporter falls back in love with her cynical managing editor while covering a Chicago jail break. (Other film versions of *The Front Page* were made under that title by Lewis Milestone in 1931 and Billy Wilder in 1974.)

1941
Sergeant York (Warner Bros.)
Production Company: Warner Bros.
Producers: Jesse L. Lasky, Hal B. Wallis.
Director: Howard Hawks.
Script: John Huston, Howard Koch, Abem Finkel, Harry Chandlee,

from *War Diary of Sergeant York*, edited by Sam K. Cowan; *Sergeant York and His People*, by Cowan; and *Sergeant York – Last of the Long Hunters*, by Tom Skeyhill.

Director of Photography: Sol Polito.

War Sequences Photographer: Arthur Edeson.

Second-Unit Director: B. Reeves Eason.

Music: Max Steiner.

Art Director: John Hughes.

Set Decorator: Fred MacLean.

Editor: William Holmes.

Running time: 134 minutes.

Released September 9, 1941, by Warner Bros.

Cast: Gary Cooper (Sgt Alvin C. York), Walter Brennan (Pastor Rosier Pile), Joan Leslie (Gracie Williams), Margaret Wycherly (Mother York), George Tobias (Michael T. 'Pusher' Ross), Stanley Ridges (Major Buxton), Ward Bond (Ike Botkin), Noah Beery, Jr (Buck Lipscomb), June Lockhart (Rosie York), Dickie Moore (George York), Clem Bevans (Zeke), Howard da Silva (Lem), Charles Trowbridge (Cordell Hull), Harvey Stevens (Captain Danforth), David Bruce (Bert Thomas), Charles Esmond (German major), Joseph Sawyer (Sgt Early), Pat Flaherty (Sgt Harry Parsons), Robert Porterfield (Zeb Andrews), Erville Alderson (Nate Tompkins), Frank Wilcox (sergeant), Donald Douglas (Captain Tillman), Lane Chandler (Cpl Savage), Frank Marlowe (Beardsley), Jack Pennick (Cpl Cutting), James Anderson (Eb), Guy Wilkerson (Tom), Tully Marshall (Uncle Lige), Lee 'Lasses' White (Luke, the target keeper), Charles Middleton (mountaineer), Victor Kilian (Andrews), Theodore Von Eltz (prison camp commander), Jane Isbell (Gracie's sister), Frank Orth (drummer), Arthur Aylesworth (Marter, the bartender), Elisha Cook, Jr (piano player), William Haade (card player), Joseph Girard (General John Pershing), Jean Del Val (Marshal Foch), Douglas Wood (Mayor Hylan), Ed Keane (Oscar of the Waldorf), Ray Teal (soldier).

The disillusionment of Alvin York, a Tennessee mountain man who abandons his pacifist convictions, fights in World War I, and becomes a national hero. (Hawks received his only Academy

Award nomination as best director, losing to John Ford for *How Green Was My Valley*; Cooper won an Oscar for best actor, and William Holmes for editing.)

1942
Ball of Fire (United Artists)
Production Company: Goldwyn Productions.
Producer: Samuel Goldwyn.
Director: Howard Hawks.
Script: Billy Wilder, Charles Brackett, from the story 'From A to Z', by Wilder and Thomas Monroe.
Director of Photography: Gregg Toland.
Art Director: Perry Ferguson.
Music: Alfred Newman.
Editor: Daniel Mandell.
Running time: 111 minutes.
Released January 9, 1942, by United Artists.
Cast: Gary Cooper (Professor Bertram Potts), Barbara Stanwyck (Sugarpuss O'Shea), Oscar Homolka (Professor Gurkakoff), Dana Andrews (Joe Lilac), Dan Duryea (Duke Pastrami), Henry Travers (Professor Jerome), S. Z. Sakall (Professor Magenbruch), Tully Marshall (Professor Robinson), Leonid Kinsky (Professor Quintana), Richard Haydn (Professor Oddly), Aubrey Mather (Professor Peagram), Allen Jenkins (garbage man), Ralph Peters (Asthma Anderson), Kathleen Howard (Miss Bragg), Mary Field (Miss Totten), Charles Lane (Larsen), Charles Arnt (McNeary), Elisha Cook, Jr (waiter), Alan Rhoin (Horseface), Eddie Foster (Pinstripe), Aldrich Bowker (justice of the peace), Addison Richards (district attorney), Pat West (bum), Kenneth Howell (college boy), Tommy Ryan (newsboy), Tim Ryan (motorcycle cop), Will Lee (Benny The Creep), Otto Hoffmann (stage doorman), Pat Flaherty, George Sherwood (deputies), Geraldine (Fissette), and Gene Krupa and His Band.

The sanctuary of eight professors working on an encyclopaedia is disrupted by a nightclub singer recruited to help with an entry on slang. (Remade by Hawks in 1948 as the musical *A Song is Born*.)

1943
Air Force (Warner Bros.)

Production Company: Warner Bros.
Producer: Hal B. Wallis.
Director: Howard Hawks.
Script: Dudley Nichols (and William Faulkner, uncredited).
Director of Photography: James Wong Howe.
Aerial Photography: Elmer Dyer, Charles Marshall.
Chief Pilot: Paul Mantz.
Second-Unit Director: B. Reeves Eason.
Art Director: John Hughes.
Set Decorator: Walter F. Tilford.
Music: Franz Waxman.
Costumes: Milo Anderson.
Editor: George Amy.
Assistant Director: Jack Sullivan.
Running time: 124 minutes.
Released March 20, 1943, by Warner Bros.
Cast: John Garfield (Sgt John B. Winocki), John Ridgely (Captain Michael A. Quincannon), Harry Carey (Sgt R. L. White), Gig Young (Lt Xavier W. Williams), George Tobias (Cpl B. B. Weinberg), Arthur Kennedy (Lt T. C. McMartin), James Brown (Lt T. A. Rader), Ray Montgomery (H. W. Chester), Charles Drake (Lt M. W. Hauser), Ward Wood (Cpl Gus Peterson), Moroni Olsen, Stanley Ridges, Willard Robertson, Edward S. Brophy, Richard Lane, Bill Crago, Faye Emerson, Addison Richards, James Flavin, Ann Doran, Dorothy Peterson.

The saga of a B-17 bomber, the 'Mary Ann', and the men who flew her in the Pacific Theater during the early days of America's involvement in World War II. (Academy Award to editor George Amy.)

1945
To Have and Have Not (Warner Bros.)

Production Company: Warner Bros.
Producer: Howard Hawks.

Director: Hawks.
Script: Jules Furthman, William Faulkner, from the novel by Ernest Hemingway.
Director of Photography: Sid Hickox.
Art Director: Charles Novi.
Set Decoration: Casey Roberts.
Music: Max Steiner.
Songs: Hoagy Carmichael, Johnny Mercer.
Editor: Christian Nyby.
Technical Advisor: Louis Comien.
Assistant Director: Jack Sullivan.
Running time: 100 minutes.
Released January 20, 1945, by Warner Bros.
Cast: Humphrey Bogart (Harry Morgan), Lauren Bacall (Marie Browning, called 'Slim'), Walter Brennan (Eddie), Hoagy Carmichael (Cricket), Dan Seymour (Captain Renard), Marcel Dalio (Gérard, called 'Frenchy'), Walter Molnar (Paul de Bursac), Dolores Moran (Hélene de Bursac), Sheldon Leonard (Lt Coyo), Walter Sande (Johnson), Aldo Nadi (bodyguard), Paul Marion (Beauclerc), Patricia Shay (Mrs Beauclerc), Pat West (bartender), Emmett Smith (Emil), Janette Grae (Rosalie), Sir Lancelot (Horatio), Eugene Borden (quartermaster), Elzie Emanuel, Harold Garrison (children), Pedro Regas (civilian), Major Fred Farrell (headwaiter), Adrienne d'Ambricourt (cashier), Hal Kelly (detective), Ron Randell (ensign), Audrey Armstrong (dancer), Marguerita Sylva (cashier), Chef Joseph Milani (chef), Maurice Marsao, Fred Dosch, George Suzanne, Louis Mercier, Crane Whitley (DeGaullists).

Hard-boiled privateer Harry Morgan comes to the aid of the Free French movement in Martinique during World War II. (Remade as *The Breaking Point* by Michael Curtiz in 1950 and as *The Gun Runners* by Don Siegel in 1958.)

1946
The Big Sleep (Warner Bros.)
Production Company: Warner Bros.
Producer: Howard Hawks.

Director: Hawks.
Script: William Faulkner, Leigh Brackett, Jules Furthman, from the novel by Raymond Chandler.
Director of Photography: Sid Hickox.
Music: Max Steiner.
Art Director: Carl Jules Weyl.
Set Decorator: Fred M. MacLean.
Editor: Christian Nyby.
Assistant Director: Chuck Hansen.
Running time: 114 minutes.
Released August 31, 1946, by Warner Bros.
Cast: Humphrey Bogart (Philip Marlowe), Lauren Bacall (Vivian Sternwood Rutledge), John Ridgely (Eddie Mars), Martha Vickers (Carmen Sternwood), Dorothy Malone (girl in bookshop), Peggy Knudsen (Mona Mars), Regis Toomey (Bernie Ohls), Charles Waldron (Gen Sternwood), Charles D. Brown (Morris, the butler), Bob Steele (Canino), Elisha Cook, Jr (Harry Jones), Louis Jean Heydt (Joe Brody), Sonia Darrin (Agnes Lowzier), Theodore Von Eltz (Arthur Gwynne Geiger), Tom Raffery (Carol Lundgren), James Flavin (Captain Cronjager), Joseph Crehan (medical examiner), Joy Barlowe (taxi driver), Tom Fadden (Sidney), Ben Welden (Pete), Trevor Bardette (Art Huck), Emmett Vogan (Ed, the deputy), Forbes Murray (furtive man), Pete Kooy (motorcycle cop), Carole Douglas (librarian), Jack Chefe (croupier), Paul Weber, Jack Perry, Wally Walker (Mars's thugs), Lorraine Miller (hat check girl), Shelby Payne (cigarette girl), Janis Chandler, Deannie Bert (waitresses), Marc Lawrence.

Philip Marlowe, a private dick on a hot case, keeps his cool with the help of a sultry sidekick. (Remade in 1977 by Michael Winner.)

1948
Red River (United Artists)
Production Company: Monterey Productions.
Producer: Howard Hawks.
Director: Hawks.
Associate Director: Arthur Rosson.

Script: Borden Chase, Charles Schnee, from Chase's magazine serial 'The Chisholm Trail'.
Director of Photography: Russell Harlan.
Art Director: John Datu Arensma.
Music: Dimitri Tiomkin.
Editor: Christian Nyby.
Running time: 125 minutes.
Released August 20, 1948, by United Artists.
Cast: John Wayne (Tom Dunson), Montgomery Clift (Matthew Garth), Joanne Dru (Tess Millay), Walter Brennan (Groot Nadine), Coleen Gray (Fen), John Ireland (Cherry Valance), Noah Beery, Jr (Buster McGee), Chief Yowlachie (Quo), Harry Carey, Sr (Melville), Harry Carey, Jr (Dan Latimer), Mickey Kuhn (Matthew as a boy), Paul Fix (Teeler Yacey), Hank Worden (Simms), Ivan Parry (Bunk Kenneally), Hal Taliaferro (Old Leather), Paul Fiero (Fernandez), Billy Self (wounded wrangler), Ray Hyke (Walt Jergens), Tom Tyler (quitter), Lane Chandler (colonel), Glenn Strange (Naylor), Shelley Winters (dance hall girl).

Tom Dunson leads the historic cattle drive along the Chisholm Trail, but his tyrannical behaviour causes his men and his adopted son to mutiny.

1948
A Song Is Born (United Artists)
Production Company: Goldwyn Productions.
Producer: Samuel Goldwyn.
Director: Howard Hawks.
Script: Harry Tugend, from the screenplay *Ball of Fire*, by Billy Wilder and Charles Brackett, based on the story 'From A to Z', by Wilder and Thomas Monroe.
Director of Photography: Gregg Toland (in Technicolor).
Music: Emil Newman, Hugo Friedhofer.
Songs: Don Raye, Gene DePaul.
Editor: Daniel Mandell.
Running time: 113 minutes.
Released November 6, 1948, by United Artists.

Cast: Danny Kaye (Professor Robert Frisbee), Virginia Mayo (Honey Swanson), Benny Goodman (Professor Magenbruch), Hugh Herbert (Professor Swingle), Steve Cochran (Tony Crow), J. Edward Bromberg (Dr Elfini), Felix Bressart (Professor Gurkakoff), Ludwig Stossel (Professor Traumer), O. Z. Whitehead (Professor Oddly), Esther Dale (Miss Bragg), Mary Field (Miss Totten), Howland Chamberlain (Setter), Paul Langton (Joe), Sidney Blackmer (Adams), Ben Weldon (Monte), Ben Chasen (Ben), Peter Virgo (Louis), and Tommy Dorsey, Louis Armstrong, Lionel Hampton, Charlie Barnet, Mel Powell, Buck and Bubbles, The Page Cavanaugh Trio, The Golden Gate Quartet, and Russo and the Samba Kings.

A musical remake of *Ball of Fire*, with Danny Kaye as a musicologist researching jazz.

1949
I Was A Male War Bride (Twentieth Century-Fox)
Production Company: Twentieth Century-Fox.
Producer: Sol C. Siegel.
Director: Howard Hawks.
Script: Charles Lederer, Leonard Spigelgass, Hagar Wilde, from a story by Henri Rochard.
Directors of Photography: Norbert Brodine, O. H. Borrodaile.
Art Directors: Lyle Wheeler, Albert Hogsett.
Set Decorators: Thomas Little, Walter M. Scott.
Music: Cyril Mockridge.
Editor: James B. Clark.
Assistant Director: Arthur Jacobson.
Running time: 105 minutes.
Released September 1949, by Twentieth Century-Fox.
Cast: Cary Grant (Captain Henri Rochard), Ann Sheridan (Lt Catherine Gates), William Neff (Captain Jack Rumsey), Eugene Gericke (Tony Jewitt), Marion Marshall (Kitty), Randy Stuart (Mae), Ruben Wendorf (innkeeper's assistant), Lester Sharpe (waiter), Ken Tobey (seaman), Robert Stevenson (lieutenant), Alfred Linder (bartender), David McMahon (chaplain), Joe Haworth

(shore patrol), John Whitney (Trumble), William Pullen, Billy Self (sergeants), Otto Relchow (German policeman), William Yetter (second German policeman), Andre Charlot (French minister), Alex Gerry (waiter), Russ Conway (Commander Willis), Harry Lauter (lieutenant), Kay Young (Major Prendergast), Lillie Kann (innkeeper's wife), Carl Jaffe (jail officer), Martin Miller (Schindler), Paul Hardmuth (burgermeister), John Serrett (French notary), Bill Murphy (soldier).

A French officer marries an American officer in post-World War II Germany and has to disguise himself as a woman in order to accompany her to the United States. (British title: *You Can't Sleep Here.*)

1952
The Big Sky (RKO)
Production Company: Winchester Productions.
Producer: Howard Hawks.
Director: Hawks.
Second-Unit Director: Arthur Rosson.
Script: Dudley Nichols, from the novel by A. B. Guthrie, Jr.
Director of Photography: Russell Harlan.
Music: Dimitri Tiomkin.
Songs: Gordon Clark.
Art Directors: Albert S. D'Agostino, Perry Ferguson.
Set Decorators: Darrell Silvera, William Stevens.
Editor: Christian Nyby.
Costumes: Dorothy Jeakins.
Assistant Director: William McGarry.
Running time: 140 minutes.
Released August 1952, by RKO.
Cast: Kirk Douglas (Jim Deakins), Dewey Martin (Boone Caudell), Elizabeth Coyote Threatt (Teal Eye), Arthur Hunnicutt (Zeb), Buddy Baer (Romaine), Steven Geray (Jourdonnais), Hank Worden (Poordevil), Jim Davis (Streak), Henri Letondal (Labadie), Robert Hunter (Chouquette), Booth Colman (Pascal), Paul Frees (McMasters), Frank De Cova (Moleface), Guy Wilkerson (Longface), Don

Beddoe (townsman), Barbara Hawks (Indian girl).

Two men on a keelboat voyage up the Missouri River in 1830 are separated by their love for an Indian girl.

1952
The Ransom of Red Chief (an episode in O. *Henry's Full House*, Twentieth Century-Fox)

Production Company: Twentieth Century-Fox.
Producer: Andre Hakim.
Director: Howard Hawks.
Script: Nunnally Johnson, from the story by O. Henry.
Director of Photography: Milton Krasner.
Art Director: Chester Goce.
Music: Alfred Newman.
Running time: 21 minutes (of the film's total running time of 106 minutes).
Released September 1952, by Twentieth Century-Fox.
Cast: Fred Allen (Sam), Oscar Levant (Bill), Lee Aaker (J. B.), Kathleen Freeman (J. B.'s mother), Alfred Miner (J. B.'s father).

Two gangsters kidnap a little boy, who is so obnoxious that they pay his parents to take him back. (The fourth episode in a five-part film [others were directed by Henry Hathaway, Jean Negulesco, and Henry King], Hawks's sketch was later cut from the film on the [accurate] grounds that it was not funny.)

1952
Monkey Business (Twentieth Century-Fox)

Production Company: Twentieth Century-Fox.
Producer: Sol C. Siegel.
Director: Howard Hawks.
Script: Ben Hecht, I. A. L. Diamond, Charles Lederer, from a story by Harry Segall.
Director of Photography: Milton Krasner.
Music: Leigh Harline.
Art Directors: Lyle Wheeler, George Patrick.
Set Decorators: Thomas Little, Walter M. Scott.

Costumes: Charles Le Maire, Travilla.
Editor: William B. Murphy.
Running time: 97 minutes.
Released September 1952, by Twentieth Century-Fox.
Cast: Cary Grant (Professor Barnaby Fulton), Ginger Rogers (Edwina Fulton), Charles Coburn (Oliver Oxly), Marilyn Monroe (Lois Laurel), Hugh Marlowe (Hank Entwhistle), Henri Letondal (Dr Siegfried Kitzel), Robert Cornthwaite (Dr Zoldeck), Larry Keating (O. J. Gulverly), Douglas Spencer (Dr Bruner), Esther Dale (Mrs Rhinelander), George Winslow (deep-voiced boy), Emmett Lynn (Jimmy), Kathleen Freeman (Mrs Brannigan), Harry Carey, Jr, Jerry Sheldon (detectives), Howard Hawks (off-screen voice in opening scene).

A scientist and his wife revert to childhood when they drink a youth potion accidentally invented by a chimpanzee.

1953
Gentlemen Prefer Blondes (Twentieth Century-Fox)
Production Company: Twentieth Century-Fox.
Producer: Sol C. Siegel.
Director: Howard Hawks.
Script: Charles Lederer, from the musical by Anita Loos and Joseph Fields, based on the novel by Loos.
Director of Photography: Harry J. Wild (in Technicolor).
Art Directors: Lyle Wheeler, Joseph C. Wright.
Musical Direction: Lionel Newman.
Songs: Jule Styne, Leo Robin, Hoagy Carmichael, Harold Adamson.
Choreography: Jack Cole.
Costumes: Travilla.
Editor: Hugh S. Fowler.
Assistant Director: Paul Helmick.
Running time: 91 minutes.
Released August 1953, by Twentieth Century-Fox.
Cast: Jane Russell (Dorothy Shaw), Marilyn Monroe (Lorelei Lee), Charles Coburn (Sir Francis Beekman), Elliott Reid (Malone),

Tommy Noonan (Gus Esmond), George Winslow (Henry Spofford III), Marcel Dalio (magistrate), Taylor Holmes (Esmond Sr), Norma Varden (Lady Beekman), Howard Wendell (Watson), Steven Geray (hotel manager), Peter Camlin (gendarme), Henri Letondal (Grotier), Leo Mostovoy (Phillippe), Alex Frazer (Pritchard), George Dee, Jimmy Saung, George Chakiris (dancers), George Davis (taxi driver), Alphonse Martell (headwaiter), Jimmie Moultrie, Freddie Moultrie (boy dancers), Harry Carey, Jr (Winslow), Jean Del Val (ship's captain), Ray Montgomery (Peters), Alvy Moore (Anderson), Robert Nichols (Evans), Charles Tannen (Ed), Jimmy Young (Stevens), Charles De Ravenne (purser), John Close (coach), William Cabanne (Sims), Philip Sylvestre (steward), Alfred Paix (porter), Max Willenz (court clerk), Rolfe Sedan (waiter), Robert Foulk, Ralph Peters (passport officials), Harry Seymour (captain of waiters), Robert Fuller.
Two floozie chantoozies at large in Gay Paree.

1955
Land of the Pharaohs (Warner Bros.)
Production Company: Continental Productions.
Producer: Howard Hawks.
Associate Producer: Arthur Siteman.
Director: Hawks.
Second-Unit Director: Noël Howard.
Script: William Faulkner, Harry Kurnitz, Harold Jack Bloom.
Directors of Photography: Lee Garmes, Russell Harlan (in Cinema-Scope and Warner-color).
Art Director: Alexandre Trauner.
Music: Dimitri Tiomkin.
Costumes: Mayo.
Editor: V. Sagovsky, supervised by Rudi Fehr.
Assistant Directors: Paul Helmick, Jean-Paul Sassy.
Assistant to the Second-Unit Director: Chuck Hansen.
Running time: 106 minutes.
Released July 2, 1955, by Warner Bros.
Cast: Jack Hawkins (Pharaoh Cheops), Joan Collins (Princess Nellifer), Dewey Martin (Senta), Alexis Minotis (Hamar), James

Robertson Justice (Vashtar), Luisa Boni (Kyra), Sydney Chaplin (Trench), James Hayter (Mikka, Vashtar's servant), Kerima (Queen Nailla), Piero Giagnoni (Prince Zanin), Carlo d'Angelo (overseer).

A pharaoh's obsessive desire to achieve immortality by building a pyramid.

1959
Rio Bravo (Warner Bros.)
Production Company: Armada Productions.
Producer: Howard Hawks.
Director: Hawks.
Script: Jules Furthman, Leigh Brackett, from a story by B. H. McCampbell (Barbara Hawks McCampbell).
Director of Photography: Russell Harlan (in Technicolor).
Music: Dimitri Tiomkin.
Songs: Tiomkin, Paul Francis Webster.
Art Director: Leo K. Kuter.
Set Decorator: Ralph S. Hurst.
Costumes: Marjorie Best.
Editor: Folmar Blangsted.
Assistant Director: Paul Helmick.
Running time: 141 minutes.
Released April 4, 1959, by Warner Bros.
Cast: John Wayne (Sheriff John T. Chance), Dean Martin (Dude), Ricky Nelson (Colorado Ryan), Angie Dickinson (Feathers), Walter Brennan (Stumpy), Ward Bond (Pat Wheeler), John Russell (Nathan Burdett), Pedro Gonzalez-Gonzalez (Carlos Remonte), Claude Akins (Joe Burdett), Estelita Rodriguez (Consuela), Harry Carey, Jr (Harold), Malcolm Atterbury (Jake), Bob Steele (Matt Harris), Myron Healy (barfly), Fred Graham (gunman), Riley Hill (messenger), Tom Monroe (henchman), Bob Terhune (Charlie, the bartender), Ted White (Bart), Nesdon Booth (Clark), George Bruggeman (Clem), Jose Cuchillo (Pedro), Eugene Iglesias (bystander), Joseph Shimada (Burt, the funeral director).

A sheriff, his drunken deputy, a young gunfighter, a lady gambler, and a toothless old cripple join forces to defend a jail against a horde of outlaws. (Working title: *Bull by the Tail*.)

1962
Hatari! (Paramount)

Production Company: Malabar Productions.
Producer: Howard Hawks.
Director: Hawks.
Associate Producer and Second-Unit Director: Paul Helmick.
Assistant Directors: Tom Connors, Russ Saunders.
Script: Leigh Brackett, from a story by Harry Kurnitz.
Director of Photography: Russell Harlan (in Technicolor).
Associate Photographer: Joseph Brun.
Art Directors: Hal Pereira, Carl Anderson.
Set Decorators: Sam Comer, Claude E. Carpenter.
Music: Henry Mancini.
Song: Hoagy Carmichael, Johnny Mercer.
Costumes: Edith Head, Frank Beetson, Jr.
Editor: Stuart Gilmore.
Technical Advisor: Willy deBeer.
Running time: 159 minutes.
Released June 1962, by Paramount.
Cast: John Wayne (Sean Mercer), Elsa Martinelli (Anna-Maria D'Alessandro, called 'Dallas'), Hardy Kruger (Kurt Mueller), Gérard Blain (Charles Maurey, called 'Chips'), Red Buttons (Pockets), Michéle Girardon (Brandy Delacourt), Bruce Cabot (Indian), Valentin de Vargas (Luis Francisco Garcia Lopez), Eduard Franz (Dr Sanderson), Queenie Leonard (nurse), Jon Chevron (Joseph), Emmett E. Smith (bartender), Henry Scott (Sikh clerk), Jack Williams (native), Eric Rungren (Stan), Umbopa M'Beti (Arga), Koume Samburu (Saidi).

The tracking and capture of a wary hunter by a female photographer during an African expedition for zoo animals. (The title is the Swahili word for 'danger'.)

1964
Man's Favorite Sport? (Universal)
Production Company: Gibraltar-Laurel.
Producer: Howard Hawks.
Director: Hawks.
Script: John Fenton Murray, Steve McNeil, from the story 'The Girl Who Almost Got Away', by Pat Frank.
Director of Photography: Russell Harlan (in Technicolor).
Music: Henry Mancini.
Art Directors: Alexander Golitzen, Tambi Larsen.
Editor: Stuart Gilmore.
Assistant Director: Tom Connors, Jr.
Running time: 127 minutes.
Released March 1964, by Universal.
Cast: Rock Hudson (Roger Willoughby), Paula Prentiss (Abigail Page), Maria Perschy (Isolde 'Easy' Mueller), John McGiver (William Cadwalader), Charlene Holt (Tex Connors), Roscoe Karns (Major Phipps), James Westerfield (policeman), Norman Alden (John Screaming Eagle), Forrest Lewis (Skaggs), Regis Toomey (Bagley), Tyler McVey (Bush), Kathie Brown (Marcia).

A fishing expert who has never fished is forced to enter a fishing tournament, with grave results to his dignity.

1965
Red Line 7000 (Paramount)
Production Company: Laurel Productions.
Producer: Howard Hawks.
Director: Hawks.
Second-Unit Director: Bruce Kessler.
Script: George Kirgo, from a story by Hawks.
Director of Photography: Milton Krasner (in Technicolor).
Music: Nelson Riddle.
Art Directors: Hal Pereira, Arthur Lonergan.
Editors: Stuart Gilmore, Bill Brame.
Assistant Director: Dick Moder.
Running time: 127 minutes.

Released in November 1965, by Paramount.

Cast: James Caan (Mike Marsh), Laura Devon (Julie Kazarian) Gail Hire (Holly MacGregor), Charlene Holt (Lindy Bonaparte), John Robert Crawford (Ned Arp), Marianna Hill (Gabrielle 'Gaby' Queneau), James Ward (Dan McCall), Norman Alden (Pat Kazarian), George Takei (Kato), Carol Connors, Beryl Hammond, Leslie Sommers, Diane Strom, Cissy Wellman, Forrest Lewis, Dee Hartford, Anthony Rogers, Anne Morell, John Gabriel, Bob Donner.

The professional and sexual conflicts among a group of young drivers on the stock-car racing circuit.

1967
El Dorado (Paramount)

Production Company: Laurel Productions.
Producer: Howard Hawks.
Director: Hawks.
Script: Leigh Brackett, from the novel *The Stars in Their Courses*, by Harry Brown.
Director of Photography: Harold Rosson (in Technicolor).
Music: Nelson Riddle.
Art Directors: Hal Pereira, Carl Anderson.
Editor: John Woodcock.
Assistant Director: Andrew J. Durkus.
Main Title Paintings: Olaf Wieghorst.
Running time: 110 minutes.
Released June 1967, by Paramount.
Cast: John Wayne (Cole Thornton), Robert Mitchum (Sheriff J. P. Harrah), James Caan (Alan Bourdillon Traherne, called 'Mississippi'), Charlene Holt (Maudie), Michele Carey (Joey MacDonald), Arthur Hunnicutt (Bull Harris), R. G. Armstrong (Kevin MacDonald), Edward Asner (Bart Jason), Paul Fix (Doc Miller), Christopher George (Nelse McLeod), Robert Donner (Milt), John Gabriel (Pedro), Jim Davis (Jason's foreman), Marina Ghane (Maria), Anne Newman (Saul MacDonald's wife), Johnny Crawford (Luke MacDonald), Robert Rothwell (Saul MacDonald), Adam Roarke

(Matt MacDonald), Charles Courtney (Jared MacDonald), Diane Strom (Matt's wife), Victoria George (Jared's wife), Anthony Rogers (Dr Donovan), Olaf Wieghorst (Swedish gunsmith).

An aging gunfighter, crippled by a bullet lodged against his spine, rehabilitates a drunken sheriff and helps him defend his jail.

1970
Rio Lobo (Cinema Center)
Production Company: Malabar Productions-Cinema Center Films-National General.
Producer: Howard Hawks.
Associate Producer: Paul Helmick.
Director: Hawks.
Second-Unit Director: Yakima Canutt.
Script: Leigh Brackett, Burton Wohl, from a story by Wohl.
Director of Photography: William Clothier (in Technicolor).
Production Designer: Robert Smith.
Set Decorator: William Kiernan.
Costumes: Luster Bayless.
Music: Jerry Goldsmith.
Editor: John Woodcock.
Assistant Director: Mike Moder.
Technical Advisor for Train Sequence: William Byrne.
Running time: 114 minutes.
Released December 1970, by Cinema Center Films.
Cast: John Wayne (Captain Cord McNally), Jorge Rivero (Lt Pierre Cordona), Jack Elam (Phillips), Chris Mitchum (Tuscarora), Jennifer O'Neill (Shasta), Victor French (Ketcham), Mike Henry (Sheriff Hendricks), David Huddleston (Dr Jones), Peter Jason (Lt Forsythe), Susana Dosamantes (Maria Carmen), Edward Faulkner (Lt Harris), Bill Williams (Sheriff Cronin), Sherry Lansing (Amelita), Dean Smith (Bitey), Robert Donner (Whitey), Jim Davis (Riley), Robert Rothwell, Chuck Courtney, George Plimpton (Whitey's henchmen).

A former Union officer, with the help of two former Confederates, three girls, and a trigger-happy old farmer, hunts down the traitor who betrayed his men in the war.

Selected Bibliography

Bacall, Lauren. *By Myself*. New York: Knopf, 1979.

Bazin, André. 'Comment peut-on être Hitchcocko-Hawksien?' *Cahiers du Cinéma*, February 1955, pp. 17–18.

Becker, Jacques; Rivette, Jacques; and Truffaut, François. 'Howard Hawks' [interview]. *Cahiers du Cinéma*, February 1956, pp. 4–17. Reprinted in English translation in *Interviews with Film Directors*, edited by Andrew Sarris, pp. 187–196. New York: Avon Books, 1967.

Belton, John. 'Hawks and Co'. *Cinema* (UK), no. 9, 1971; reprinted in *Focus on Howard Hawks*, edited by Joseph McBride, pp. 94–108. Englewood Cliffs, N.J.: Prentice-Hall, 1972.

- *The Hollywood Professionals*. Vol. 3, *Howard Hawks, Frank Borzage, and Edgar G. Ulmer*. New York: A. S. Barnes, 1974.

Bogdanovich, Peter. *The Cinema of Howard Hawks*. New York: Museum of Modern Art Film Library, 1962. Consists of interview, reprinted in *Movie*, December 1962, pp. 8–18, and in French translation in *Cahiers du Cinéma*, January 1963, pp. 5–56, as part of a Hawks filmography, with commentary by various critics.

Bourget, Jean-Loup. 'Hawks et le mythe de l'Ouest Américain'. *Positif*, nos. 195–96 (July–August 1977), pp. 31–42.

Brackett, Leigh. 'A Comment on the Hawksian Woman'. *Take One*, July–August 1971, pp. 19–20.

Byron, Stuart, '*Auteurism*, Hawks, *Hatari!*, and Me'. In *Favorite Movies*, edited by Philip Nobile, pp. 254–67. New York: Macmillan, 1973.

Chase, Borden. In 'The Rise and Fall of the American West', by Jim Kitses [interview]. *Film Comment*, Winter 1970–71, pp. 14–21.

Ciment, Michel. 'Entretien avec Howard Hawks'. *Positif*, nos. 195–

96 (July–August 1977), pp. 50–56.

– 'Hawks et l'écrit'. *Positif*, nos. 195–96 (July–August 1977), pp. 43–49.

Comolli, Jean-Louis. 'Entretien avec Howard Hawks'. *Cahiers du Cinéma*, no. 192 (July–August 1967), pp. 17–22.

– 'Howard Hawks aujourd'hui'. *Cahiers du Cinéma*, no. 160 (November 1964), pp. 48–52.

Durgnat, Raymond. 'Durgnat vs. Paul: Last Round in the Great Hawks Debate'. *Film Comment*, March–April 1978, pp. 64–68. Rebuttal to William Paul's article 'Hawks vs. Durgnat' (see below).

– 'Hawks Isn't Good Enough'. *Film Comment*, July–August 1977, pp. 8–19.

Eyquem, Oliver. 'Howard Hawks, ingénieur'. *Positif*, nos. 195–96 (July–August 1977), pp. 6–10.

Farber, Manny. 'Howard Hawks'. *Artforum*, April 1969; reprinted in *Focus on Howard Hawks*, edited by Joseph McBride, pp. 28–34. Englewood Cliffs, N.J.: Prentice-Hall, 1972.

Faulkner, William; Brackett, Leigh; and Furthman, Jules. *The Big Sleep* [screenplay, from the novel by Raymond Chandler]. In *Film Scripts One*, edited by George P. Garrett, O. B. Hardison, Jr., and Jane R. Gelfman, pp. 137–329. New York: Appleton-Century-Crofts, 1971.

Furthman, Jules, and Faulkner, William. *To Have and Have Not* [screenplay, from the novel by Ernest Hemingway]. Edited and introduced by Bruce F. Kawin. Madison: University of Wisconsin Press, 1979.

Gallagher, John, and Sarowitz, Sam. 'Truffaut: The Man Who Loved Movies'. *Grand Illusions*, Winter 1977, pp. 26–32.

Gili, Jean A. *Howard Hawks*. Cinéma d'Aujourd'hui [series]. Paris: Editions Seghers, 1971.

Haskell, Molly. 'Howard Hawks'. In *Cinema: A Critical Dictionary*, edited by Richard Roud, Vol. 1, pp. 473–86. London: Secker and Warburg, and New York: Viking Press, 1980.

– 'Howard Hawks: Masculine Feminine'. *Film Comment*, March 1974, pp. 34–39.

Hecht, Ben; Miller, Seton I.; Mahin, John Lee; Burnett, W. R.; and

Pasley, Fred. *Scarface* [screenplay, in French translation, from the novel by Armitage Trail]. In *L'Avant-Scène du Cinéma*, no. 132 (1973), pp. 6–38.

Hotchner, A. E. *Papa Hemingway: A Personal Memoir*. New York: Random House, 1966.

Howard, Noël. *Hollywood sur Nile*. Paris: Librairie Arthème Fayard, 1978. Hawks's second-unit director's account of the making of *Land of the Pharaohs*.

Kawin, Bruce F. *Faulkner and Film*. New York: Frederick Unger, 1977.

Legrand, Gérard. 'Petit discours de la méthode de H. H.' *Positif*, nos. 195–96 (July–August 1977), pp. 11–17.

Lehman, Peter, et al. 'Howard Hawks: A Private Interview'. *Wide Angle*, Summer 1976, pp. 28–57.

McBride, Joseph, ed. *Focus on Howard Hawks*. Englewood Cliffs, N.J.: Prentice-Hall, 1972.

– 'Hawks'. *Film Comment*, March–April 1978, pp. 36–41, 70–71.

McCarthy, Todd, and McBride, Joseph. 'Bombshell Days in the Golden Age' [interview with John Lee Mahin]. *Film Comment*, March–April 1980, pp. 58–68.

Masson, Alain. 'Organiser le sensible'. *Positif*, nos. 195–96 (July–August 1977), pp. 19–30.

Missiaen, Jean-Claude. *Howard Hawks*. Classiques du Cinéma [series]. Paris: Editions Universitaires, 1966.

Paul, William. 'Hawks vs. Durgnat'. *Film Comment*, January–February 1978, pp. 68–71. Rebuttal to Raymond Durgnat's article 'Hawks Isn't Good Enough' (see above).

Perkins, V. F. 'Comedies'. *Movie*, December 1962, pp. 21–22. Reprinted as 'Hawks' Comedies' in *The Movie Reader*, edited by Ian Cameron, pp. 57–58. New York and Washington, D.C.: Praeger, 1972.

– 'Hatari!', *Movie*, December 1962, pp. 28–30. Reprinted in *The Movie Reader*, edited by Ian Cameron, pp. 61–63. New York and Washington, D.C.: Praeger, 1972.

Rivette, Jacques. 'Génie de Howard Hawks'. *Cahiers du Cinéma*, May 1953; reprinted in English translation as 'The Genius of Howard Hawks' in *Focus on Howard Hawks*, edited by Joseph

McBride, pp. 70–77. Englewood Cliffs, N.J.: Prentice-Hall, 1972.

Sarris, Andrew. 'The World of Howard Hawks'. *Films and Filming*, July and August 1962, adapted from a 1961 article by Sarris in *The New York Film Bulletin*; reprinted in *Focus on Howard Hawks*, edited by Joseph McBride, pp. 35–64. Englewood Cliffs, N.J.: Prentice-Hall, 1972.

Schickel, Richard. *The Men Who Made the Movies*. New York: Atheneum, 1975, pp. 95–128.

Shivas, Mark. 'Blondes'. *Movie*, December 1962, pp. 23–24. Reprinted in *The Movie Reader*, edited by Ian Cameron, pp. 59–60. New York and Washington, D.C.: Praeger, 1972.

Silke, James R.; Daney, Serge; and Noames, Jean-Louis. 'Entretien avec Howard Hawks'. *Cahiers du Cinéma*, November 1965, pp. 54–60.

Truffaut, François. *Les Films de ma Vie*. Paris: Flammarion, 1975. English translation by Leonard Mayhew as *The Films in My Life*. New York: Simon and Schuster, 1978. Contains reviews of *Scarface, Gentlemen Prefer Blondes,* and *Land of the Pharaohs*.

Wilde, Meta Carpenter, with Borsten, Orin. *A Loving Gentleman*. New York: Simon and Schuster, 1976. Memoir of William Faulkner by Hawks's former secretary.

Wollen, Peter. *Signs and Meaning in the Cinema*. London: Thames and Hudson, and Bloomington: Indiana University Press, 1969.

Wood, Robin. 'Hawks De-Wollenized'. In *Personal Views: Explorations in Film*. London and Bedford, Eng.: The Gordon Fraser Gallery, Ltd., 1976, pp. 191–206.

– *Howard Hawks*. London: Secker and Warburg, and New York: Doubleday, 1968.

– 'To Have (Written) and Have Not (Directed): Reflections on Authorship'. *Film Comment*, May–June 1973, pp. 30–35.

Index